A HIS

EDINBURGH

LOMOND

Lomond Books Ltd
Broxburn, EH52 5NF, Scotland
www.lomondbooks.com

Created by and copyright © 2017 Flame Tree Publishing Limited
www.flametreepublishing.com

18 20 22 21 19 17
1 3 5 7 9 10 8 6 4 2

ISBN 978-1-84204-619-7

Cover photographs:
Front: Edinburgh Castle from the Ross Fountain, Princes Street Gardens
Back: *Edinburgh Castle, from the Grassmarket* by William Leighton Leitch

A copy of the CIP data for this book is available from the British Library.

Printed in Denmark

Thanks to:
Frances Bodiam, Victoria Gerrard, Anna Groves, Catherine Taylor,
Victoria Lyle, Gemma Walters, Polly Willis and Nick Wells

Image credits:
Mary Evans: 1, 3, 11, 20, 25, 29, 52, 68, 73, 94, 109, 142, 149,
152, 180, 184, 190, 210; © Illustrated London News Ltd: 86–87; ©
Antiquarian Images: 131. TopFoto: World History Archive: 100; © Print
Collector / HIP: 170 & 192; © 2003 212. Brendan Howard: front cover.
Bridgeman Images/Private Collection/© Look and Learn: back cover.

A **HISTORY** of **EDINBURGH**

Dr Christopher McNab

Foreword by John McKay

LOMOND

Foreword

ANCIENT & MIDDLE AGES EDINBURGH

REFORMATION & ENLIGHTENMENT EDINBURGH

VICTORIAN & MODERN EDINBURGH

Parliament House

Foreword

The first time I came to Edinburgh I must have been eight or nine years old. I remember three things: that the streets were made of small grey lumps, called cobbles. That we took a (bumpy) taxi ride, which was strange, and luxurious, and metropolitan. And that the town was both very tall and very hollow, and seemed stacked in layers, all folded up on top of itself.

Edinburgh became my first big city. It saw the first flush of my adolescence (the Science Fiction Bookshop, Henderson's Salad Bar, Cinderella Rockefellers), somehow withstood the drunken racketing of my college years (the City Café, La Sorbonne, Larry's Lunchette), and listened patiently to my early attempts to write and perform (the Bedlam, the Wireworks Playground, the Crown Theatre...). Everyone's location list will be different: but if you are going to pick a city to get stuck in your head forever, like the memory of first love, then smoky, hilly, beery, stony Edinburgh is a good choice to make.

It is a divine place all year round: cold and clear in winter, eternally sunlit in spring (sunshine at 10 pm!), crowded and clubbable in its short, wet, festival-strewn summer; and so eager to start autumn that you can smell the leaves falling in mid-August.

It's strange to publish a history of this city, because the town is its own memoir: where other places erase and obliterate their past when a new idea comes along, Edinburgh habitually builds alongside – or occasionally right on top of – the old. So you can walk down the High Street from the Castle Rock (as people have been strolling since the ninth century), through a cityscape straight out of the 1600s (give or take the occasional net café), spit on the Heart of Midlothian (site of public hanging until 1819) for good luck, until eventually you will reach the upturned-boat-roofed Scottish Parliament, home to a twenty-first century ideal of self-government that we last enjoyed 300 years ago. As a town plan, it's not so much a layer cake as a trifle – lots of good stuff mixed together. Home to *Ane Satyre of the Thrie Estates*, The Oxford Bar, and *Grand Theft Auto*.

But finally and always, there is something of the Sunday afternoon about Edinburgh: it can be crammed to the rafters with people, but it steadfastly refuses to bustle (unlike frenzied New York, or scary Manchester, or cheapjack old London); and you either love this forever … or you move to Glasgow.

John McKay

Introduction

Edinburgh, as the tour companies like to assure us, is a city of ghosts. Every day large groups of tourists, sometimes 40 or 50 strong, expectantly follow their guides around the city's most menacing and evocative locations – the vaults beneath South Bridge, Mary King's Close, the cemeteries of Canongate and Greyfriars.

Whether or not you believe in the visitation of spirits, it is easy to understand where the city gets its spectral reputation. On the most ghoulish level, Edinburgh has seen epic amounts of blood and death within its streets, courtyards and wynds, often with torture as an added horror. A restrained list of some of these ghastly events includes: the execution or murder of nobles and court officials such as David Rizzio, Lord Darnley, Sir William Kirkaldy of Grange, the Earls of Morton, Montrose and Argyll; acts of social violence such as the slaying of Covenanters during the 'Killing Times' of the late seventeenth century; the grotesque series of witch burnings in the sixteenth century; visitations of the Black Death from the 1300s; and the occasional large fire thrown in for good measure.

Yet there is another, more subtle, reason for Edinburgh as a top venue for those interested in the ghostly. For all the depredations of modern building work over the last century, Edinburgh is still a city whose history lies close to the surface. The castle stands as the most visible reminder of the ages, towering over the city and speaking not only of Edinburgh's martial past, but also of its origins stretching back to the Bronze Age. Just walking along the Royal Mile takes you through some of Edinburgh's most famous districts, such as the Lawnmarket, High Street, the Canongate; buildings resonate with centuries of history, such as St Giles and, at one end of the Royal Mile, the Palace and Abbey ruins of Holyrood. Surviving tenement buildings remind of dark Old Town claustrophobia and disease (although some post-Second World War housing and tower block developments have similar connotations).

Other districts of Edinburgh make similar historical testimony, from the medieval darkness of the Old Town to the Neoclassical dignity of the New Town. This book aims to capture something of that history, taking a long journey from Iron Age hill forts through to the foundation of the modern Scottish Parliament, evoking not only Edinburgh's ghosts, but also its incessant drive into the future. It will also, of necessity, take in some of the great events that shaped both Edinburgh and the nation of Scotland itself.

Light and Shadow

Recorded impressions of Edinburgh have been, and remain, varied and colourful. Some have seen the city as a place of striking beauty and intelligence, an 'Athens of the North', while others have reeled at grim sights and smells, and beat a hasty retreat elsewhere. Two nineteenth-century commentators serve to illustrate. In 1819 J.G. Lockhart (1794–1854), the son-in-law of Sir Walter Scott, stood on Calton Hill and had a near rapturous experience of Edinburgh:

> Here we paused for a time, enjoying the majestic gloom of this most picturesque of cities. A thick blue smoke hung low upon the houses, and their outlines reposed behind on ridges of purple clouds; – the smoke,

*and the clouds, and the murky air, giving yet more extravagant bulk
and altitude to those huge strange dwellings, and increasing the power
of contrast which met our view, when a few more paces more brought
us again upon the New Town – the airy bridge – the bright green vale
below and beyond it – the skirting line of the vale on either side, the
rough crags of the Castle Rock, and the broad glare of Prince's Street,
that most superb of terraces – all beaming in the open yellow light of the
sun [...] Such was my first view of Edinburgh. I descended again into
her streets in a sort of stupor of admiration.* (From J.G. Lockhart,
Peter's Letters to his Kinsfolk, 1819)

Edinburgh was, and is, undoubtedly an impressive city, and Lockhart has a
near overwhelming encounter with its grandeur and power. Of course, the
'gloom' might appear 'majestic' from a distance, particularly if you later drift
off for an expensive lunch elsewhere, but if you happen to live in its midst
the experience could be very different. Hence another nineteenth-century
writer, Robert Louis Stevenson (1850–94), who although undoubtedly
impressed with the city also appreciated that it could be a hard world:

*But Edinburgh pays cruelly for her high seat in one of the vilest climates
under the heaven. She is liable to be beaten upon by all the winds that
blow, to be drenched with rain, to be buried in cold sea fogs out of the
east, and powdered with the snow as it comes flying southward from
the Highland hills. The weather is raw and boisterous in winter, shifty
and ungenial in summer, and downright meteorological purgatory in the
spring. The delicate die early, and I, as a survivor, among bleak winds
and plumping rain, have been sometimes tempted to envy them their fate.*
(R.L. Stevenson, *Edinburgh, Picturesque Notes*, 1878)

The sheer contrast just in opinions on Edinburgh's climate is striking, but on every level Edinburgh has, throughout its winding history, been a city of contrasts, a struggle between light and shadow. In terms of architecture and living conditions, for example, Edinburgh's broad historical split has been between the Old Town and the New Town. The Old Town, which grew outwards from the castle over centuries of sprawling development, emerged as a labyrinthine and inhospitable quarter, although this is not to deny the many places of splendour and grandeur along the Royal Mile. Lack of space pushed development upwards rather than outwards, resulting in the infamous tenements than could, in some cases, reach up to 15 storeys high, into which was crammed an ever-growing population. The sheer stink of fires, effluence and human bodies pressed into so little space earned the Old Town its nickname of 'Auld Reekie', and the area grew infamous for being a place of both vitality and depravity. Then came the New Town. Created in the north of the city, the New Town was developed on the back of Enlightenment rationalism, with low-level housing built around regular, spacious street planning. Previously, the rich and the poor, noble and base, rubbed shoulders in close proximity in the Old Town, but with the development of the New Town between 1750 and 1850, the rich now had somewhere to migrate. This movement in turn heightened the contrast of Edinburgh, now split between a Victorian Old Town sinking through under-investment and over-population, and a New Town of wealth and regularity, its inhabitants spread along avenues such as Princes Street, George Street and Queen Street.

The Good and the Bad

The contrasts in physical Edinburgh are heightened by its diversity in religious, political and ideological history. In many ways Edinburgh has sat on a series of historical faultlines that have been the cause of its regular descent into violence. As the capital of Scotland, it has experienced an awkward tension between royalism and nationalism, between crowns and parliaments at opposite ends of the United Kingdom. English kings such as Edward I attempted to suppress the city, along with the rest of Scotland, from 1296, resulting in the Scottish Wars of Independence in the thirteenth and fourteenth centuries. The Union of Crowns in 1603 by no means resolved the English/Scottish tension, as within 50 years Edinburgh's religious and civic leaders were violently resisting the impositions of Charles I, and the city became embroiled in a seemingly interminable civil war. Even after the Act of Union in 1707, a momentous event that cost Edinburgh its Parliament, the Jacobite rebellions saw the city change hands between contenders and claimants to the throne.

Inseparable from Edinburgh's political upheavals has been its religious identity. Through today's secular lens, it is hard to comprehend the sheer relevance of religious faith prior to the Enlightenment. Much of Edinburgh's religious history has been concerned with the struggle between a local Presbyterianism, which emerged from the Reformation, and royally endorsed Episcopalianism or Catholicism (to simplify excessively). The consequences of this struggle have ranged from individual executions to major wars, and left a legacy of religious suspicion between Protestant and Catholic that has residual influence in Edinburgh even today.

Yet while religion has frequently bred the most egregious forms of intolerance, Edinburgh also became one of the most remarkable cities of the Enlightenment, a city where great thinkers, writers, artists and architects such as Allan Ramsay (1686–1758), Oliver Goldsmith (1730–

74), David Hume (1711–76), Adam Smith (1723–90) and Sir Walter Scott produced work that changed the intellectual map of the world. Edinburgh also became known as a city of professionals, offering some of the best practices in law, financial services and publishing anywhere in the United Kingdom.

The shape-shifting and contrasts within Edinburgh's history make it a hard city to pin down in terms of identity. Furthermore, any study of Edinburgh's history must bring us to the fully modern city that Edinburgh is today, with all the benefits and curses that entails. What is certain, however, is that it is fascinating to engage with Edinburgh's ghosts. To find out how they lived and survived through a truly remarkable history is a journey worth taking.

ANCIENT & MIDDLE AGES

Bronze Age

Edinburgh's history has a habit of throwing up surprises. Until recently it was thought that the earliest evidence of human habitation in the area dated back to 2500 BC, evidenced by flint arrowheads discovered in the locale. Then, in 2007, archaeologists working on site at South Queensferry discovered Early Bronze Age pits, and, based on fragments of pottery in the bottom of the pits, they were able to date back the evidence to some 4,000 years ago. The purpose of the pits was probably for depositing rubbish or for burials, and other evidence indicates that the area that was to become Edinburgh was settled by a people who carved out survival from fishing or basic agriculture.

There has been plenty of other material unearthed from Edinburgh indicating the presence of Bronze Age ancestors. A flint arrowhead dating from c. 2000 BC was found by a young boy and girl on Arthur's Seat, and now rests in the Museum of Scotland. In the Broomhouse area, a 3,000-year-old *timber* structure was discovered, probably used for corralling cattle or sheep. Tests on a human skull found in a stone box grave have clarified it as that of a man aged 40–50 years old who lived in the Edinburgh area c. 2150 BC.

Added together, all the discoveries show beyond doubt that by the Bronze Age settled communities were scratching out an existence from the hard landscape that would become Edinburgh.

Iron Age

It is unclear exactly when Edinburgh Castle began its long journey to emerge as a full-scale fortified structure. We do know, however, that by the Iron Age there was a permanent settlement on Castle Rock, with clear evidence of human habitation there from the first century AD. The sophistication of the settlement is only just becoming clear. At its heart was probably a collection of wooden and earthwork buildings, and recent excavation work around the castle has revealed two enormous defensive ditches dug around the perimeter of the settlement. These ditches were on a prodigious scale – they were about 12 m (39 ft) wide and 6 m (20 ft) deep – and their location atop Castle Rock gave the settlement excellent all-round protection.

Further excavations in the Edinburgh area have unearthed the remains of an Iron Age chariot, dating to about 250 BC. (It was discovered during building work at the Edinburgh Interchange near Newbridge.) It is likely to have been a burial chariot, a possibility reinforced by the nearby Iron Age burial cairn at Huly Hill. Arthur's Seat was another site of settlement (high places were naturally attractive for their defensive qualities), and trading evidence from the Edinburgh area also indicates commercial interactions with the Romans (*see* 'Arrival of the Romans', p.24).

What is clear is that by the Iron Age, people were putting down fixed roots in the Edinburgh area, sowing the seeds for the future.

Dunedin and Votadini

While it is impossible to say for certain what range of peoples was living in the Edinburgh area during the Iron Age, we do have evidence for one particular tribe, the Votadini. The Votadini spread themselves fairly widely – their territory stretched from the Firth of Forth down to the River Tyne, now part of England. The precise origins of the Votadini are now lost in the mists of time, but there is a possibility that they were inhabiting the Edinburgh area as far back as 2000 BC (*see* 'Bronze Age', p.22). A building of which the Votadini were particularly fond was the *oppidium*, or hill fort, and evidence of these structures is found on high ground throughout much of south-east Scotland. Their capital was initially Trapain Law in East Lothian (located a few miles to the east of Haddington), but there is evidence that sometime around 400 BC they shifted their centre of power to Dunedin (*Din Eidin* in Gaelic), the modern-day Edinburgh area. Here they occupied Castle Rock, and it is notable that the Roman writer Ptolemy (*c.* AD 83–161) refers in his writings to the settlement of the Votadini as 'rock place'. The descendants of the Votadini would be known during the medieval period as the Gododdin, and for a time their territory would be absorbed into the Roman province of Britannia (*see* 'Arrival of the Romans', below).

Arrival of the Romans

By AD 80 the Votadini and the many other tribes of Scotland would have been aware of a new power to the south that threatened their territorial authority. In AD 43 the Romans had landed in force in what is today southern England, and over the next three decades they steadily brought more of the land under their control, creeping northwards towards Scotland and establishing their colony of Britannia. In 79 the Roman governor Agricola began sending naval survey parties to map out the Scottish coastline prior to invasions of southern Scottish territory in the early 80s. For the Votadini in the Edinburgh area, life was about to change tremendously. Previously a fiercely independent people, they fell

under Roman rule during the second century and remained that way for nearly 30 years, later sandwiched between two major Roman fortification systems – Hadrian's Wall and the Antonine Wall. Eventually, the problems the Romans faced in quashing Caledonian rebellion resulted in the more southerly Hadrian's Wall becoming the northernmost frontier, thereby putting the Votadini outside of direct Roman control. However, trading relations with the Romans were nothing if not profitable, so the Votadini maintained commercial connections, as evidenced by the large amounts of Roman pottery and other consumer goods found around Edinburgh settlements of this period. These relations only came to a close when Rome abandoned Britain as a colony in 400.

The Picts

One of the many Scottish peoples that caused trouble for the Romans were the Picts. In essence they were a collection of tribes occupying what is now eastern and north-eastern Scotland. The Picts did not use this name themselves – the name 'Pict' first crops up in Roman literature, the word deriving from the Roman *Picti*, meaning 'painted or tattooed people', a reference to the Picts' body art.

The Romans observed the Picts as fierce and resilient enemies, and although they managed to inflict some heavy defeats on the Picts (such as at the battle of Mons Graupius in 84) they were never able to fully overcome Pictish resistance. Indeed, the Roman Antonine Wall, built in 140–42 and stretching 60 km (37 miles) from the Forth to the Clyde, formed a buttress against the southernmost extent of Pictish territory, and by 211 the Romans had pulled back even further south, to Hadrian's Wall.

For over two centuries the Picts were a thorn in the Romans' side, with frequent cross-border raids into Roman territory. The Picts would also impact upon the territory of the Votadini tribe, particularly on the Edinburgh area. Once the Romans had pulled back to Hadrian's Wall, the Picts extended their reach further south, using the Edinburgh settlements and defences as bases and strongholds. In the fifth century (probably around 452) however, the Picts established a fortress on the site of Edinburgh Castle, almost literally laying the cornerstones for the development of the rest of the city.

King Arthur

To the east of Edinburgh Castle, set in the grounds of Holyrood Park, is the 215-m (853-ft) high hill known as Arthur's Seat, after the legendary figure of King Arthur. Unpicking fact from fiction is virtually an impossibility regarding this enigmatic historical figure, but his connections with Scotland are tangible. A sixth-century poem called Y Gododin – Gododdin being the name given by the early Britons to the Votadini who inhabited the Edinburgh area from the Iron Age – makes a reference to King Arthur, indicating that his identity was well known in the locale by the early medieval period. More specifically, Geoffrey of Monmouth (c. 1100–55) related one of Arthur's battles as Monte Agned: Edinburgh Castle was, during the medieval period, known as Castelh Mynyd Agned ('the fortress of the hill of Agnes'). Arthur's Seat, however, is often held as the site of the battle, hence its title. Edinburgh Castle itself appears in several notable Arthurian tales, where it is also known as the *Castellum Puellarum* ('Castle of Maidens'). The origins of this term are uncertain, but some legends suggest that the daughters of Pictish kings were sent to the castle to receive their education in the ways of men. Other legends talk of women being held prisoner in the castle, or of siren-like temptresses who attempted to lure dutiful knights into the castle. Whatever the reality, Arthur remains part of the fabric of Edinburgh's mythical history.

The Angles of Northumbria

The Angles came to northern Britain along with the Romans, and were originally from Holstein, northern Germany. They were a combative people (they allied themselves with the Romans as auxiliary troops) and remained in Britain even after the Romans had departed, expanding from an initial base to form three major kingdoms – *Nord Angelnen* (Northumbria), *Ost Angelnen* (East Anglia), and the *Mittlere Angelnen* (Mercia). It was during the seventh century that the Angles turned their attention even further north and the fortified settlement of Dunedin fell under their gaze.

Some time after 627 the Angles launched an invasion northwards led by King Edwin (584–633), but in 638 we come across a direct reference to an assault on Edinburgh itself. The document, known as 'The siege of Eten', talks of a military action to take *Eten* – Dunedin – under the leadership of King Oswald (605–42). Dunedin and its fortress fell to the Angles, who consolidated the position and used it for further forays north and west into the Scottish hinterlands.

One of the critical effects of the Angles upon Edinburgh was in terms of its naming. The Angles translated the Gaelic words *Din Eidin* into Edinburgh, which roughly translates as an Old English version of 'fort of Eidin'. (The 'burgh' part of the expression means 'fortress' or 'walled buildings'.) As such, the Angles left Edinburgh with arguably its most profound legacy – its name.

Indulf (r. 954–62)

Indulf (Gaelic: *Idulb mac Causantín*) was one of the early kings of Alba, Alba being a Gaelic name for the country of Scotland. He was preceded by Malcolm I (c. 900–54), whose reign had ended in his bloody murder in 954. The position of king was obviously attended by great risks, but Indulf was a true warrior and he would hold the troubled throne for a total of eight years.

When Indulf came to power Edinburgh was in the hands of the Northumbrians, who had taken the fortress settlement in 638 (*see* 'The Angles of Northumbria', p.28). Two years into Indulf's reign, however, he began a programme of expansion to claw territories back into Scottish hands. By this time the Northumbrians were thoroughly ensconced in Edinburgh, and it would take considerable effort to eject them from the region. Malcolm I had himself taken on the Northumbrians during his reign, launching raiding parties that managed to push down as far as the River Tweed. Indulf's achievements, however, were more permanent. Under the force of his offensive, the Northumbrians were forced to abandon Edinburgh and retreat southwards, leaving the settlement in Scottish hands. Indulf was ultimately to die a warrior's death. With the Northumbrians expelled, Indulf then had to face the depredations of the Vikings on the Scottish coastline. In 962, at the mouth of the River Cowie, he was killed in battle.

Malcolm II (r. 1005–34)

For much of its first millennium, Edinburgh found itself in troubles. So often it rested on or near the faultlines that ran between different peoples and tribes – Votadini and Romans, Picts and Romans, Scots and Angles. Malcolm II ascended to the throne of Alba in 1005 on the death of Kenneth III (r. 997–1005), and was immediately faced with long-standing threats from the Angles further south. While history has titled him king of Scotland, in reality his authority over the territory that we know today as Scotland was partial, and large areas of Lothian remained in the possession of the Angles.

In 1018, however, the two rivals came to major blows at the Battle of Carham, fought by the banks of the River Tweed. Malcolm himself was the commander of the Scottish forces, and a contemporary account (the *Historia Ecclesiae Dunelmensis*) describes the engagement in ominous terms:

> In the year of our Lord's incarnation ten hundred and eighteen, while Cnut ruled the kingdom of the Angles, a comet appeared for thirty nights to the people of Northumbria, a terrible presage of the calamity by which that province was about to be desolated. For, shortly afterwards, (that is, after thirty days,) nearly the whole population, from the river Tees to the Tweed, and their borders, were cut off in a conflict in which they were engaged with a countless multitude of Scots at Carrun [Carham].

Malcolm secured victory at Carham, and as a result Lothian passed securely into Scottish control. Two years later Malcolm placed Edinburgh permanently under his dominion.

Malcolm III 'Canmore' (r. 1057-93)

Malcolm III 'Canmore' (meaning ' big head' or 'leader') took the title King of the Scots in 1057, his father having been killed by Macbeth (r. 1040–57) in 1040. In an act of survival, the young Malcolm pushed further south into England and returned with an army in 1054 to defeat Macbeth at the battle of Dunsinnan, and then kill him at the battle of Lumphanan in 1057. Malcolm had then to defeat Macbeth's stepson and cousin, Lulach, to secure the throne of Scotland for himself and give his lands some security.

Edinburgh became the seat of Malcolm's power and this was represented by changes he made in the structure of Edinburgh Castle. While previously the castle had been reliant upon wood for many of its defences, during the reign of Malcolm III the castle began the transition to permanent stone fortress. From this base Malcolm was faced with a growing emergency, that of the spreading Norman conquest led by William the Conqueror (c. 1027–c. 1087). The Anglo-Saxon royal family of Edgar Atheling (c. 1051–c. 1126) had fled to Scotland in the face of this conquest in 1070, and Malcolm later made raiding expeditions down into Northumbria in defiance of William's authority. Yet in 1072 William made a bold thrust into Scotland, and following a string of defeats Malcolm was forced to relent before the Normans at the Submission of Abernethy in 1072. Nonetheless, Malcolm was repeatedly embroiled in battles across the English-Scottish border, and on 13 November 1093 he was killed at the Battle of Alnwick.

Queen Margaret (c. 1045–93)

Queen Margaret was renowned for her piety and total devotion to faith, and the spirituality of her life led to her canonization in 1250 – she is Scotland's only royal saint. Such a vaunted position has testimony across Edinburgh, for example St Margaret's Chapel (located within Edinburgh Castle), St Margaret's Well and St Margaret's Loch. The lady herself was daughter of Edward (1016–57), son of Edmund Ironside (r. April–November 1016), and the sister of Edgar Atheling, the nominal English king who was forced to flee to Scotland in the face of the Norman conquest. It was in Edinburgh, under protective custody, that Margaret married the Scottish king, Malcolm III.

Margaret brought the practices of the English and European religions to Edinburgh, and was a significant reforming influence over Scottish religious practice (although this influence is often much exaggerated). A key physical addition that Margaret made to Edinburgh was the building of what is now known as St Margaret's Chapel (*see* p.34) in the upper levels of the castle; the oldest existing part of the castle.

Another aspect of Margaret's canonization may well be her marital devotion, which expressed itself in the very nature of her death. In 1093, having just been given the message informing her of Malcolm's death at the Battle of Alnwick, Margaret herself expired shortly afterwards in Edinburgh Castle, a model of devotion to the very end.

Donald Bane (r. 1093-97)

One person amongst many who was far from pleased with Malcolm III's submitting to the Normans in 1072 was his brother Donald, known to history as Donald Bane. Donald was born around 1033, and he spent some of his early years in the Hebrides, where he picked up far more northern influences than those of the Normans or the English practices brought into the Scottish court by Queen Margaret.

In 1093 Malcolm was killed at the Battle of Alnwick, and Queen Margaret quickly succumbed to serious illness. Now was the time for Donald to act. Malcolm's children had also gathered around their mother in Edinburgh Castle, so almost all of Donald's dynastic threats were gathered in one place. Gathering a force of Highlanders, Donald surrounded Edinburgh Castle with the intention of taking all his nephews prisoner. Yet this was not to be: the children managed to escape from his clutches and fled to England. Donald consequently took over Edinburgh Castle and the throne of Scotland, yet in 1094 he was militarily defeated by Malcolm's son Duncan (r. 1094), who had the backing of William the Conqueror. This was not the end of the matter, however, as Duncan himself was in killed in battle and Donald returned to the throne, only to be once again defeated in 1097 by another of Malcolm and Margaret's sons, Edgar (r. 1097–1104), who eventually had Donald incarcerated and blinded. The troubled ex-king died in 1099.

St Margaret's Chapel

Queen Margaret (*see* p.32) not only brought to Edinburgh new spiritual practices, she also was deeply interested in modern church architecture, particularly those of Norman style. (Her pet projects included the restoration of the monastery at Iona.) Standing as the oldest surviving part of Edinburgh Castle, St Margaret's Chapel was either built during her lifetime, or constructed by her son, David I, as a memorial after her death. The chapel itself is small and unpretentious, it being little more than an enclosed stone building with plain walls and a simple arch leading through to an ascetic altar. It is nevertheless a serene and harmonious place, and seems to have made an impression on all those who came into contact with it. When the English took Edinburgh Castle in 1313 (*see* 'Reclaiming the Castle', p.47), the subsequent destruction of the castle's battlements and defences did not include the venerated Chapel. Later, Robert the Bruce gave orders even as he lay dying that the Chapel was to be strictly maintained.

By the sixteenth century, however, the Chapel had become neglected, and was even re-purposed as a gunpowder magazine. It was not until the mid-nineteenth century that Victorian authorities recognized the criminality of ignoring such a beautiful building, and in 1853 restoration work on the Chapel was completed, once more revealing a place of unique spiritual beauty.

St Giles' Kirk

The story of the High Kirk of St Giles, which sits on Edinburgh's Royal Mile, is one of drama, incident and powerful figures. Documented evidence indicates a parish church in Edinburgh called St Giles (the patron saint of the city) dating back to the ninth century. The origins of the church, however, are pinpointed to the 1120s, when it emerged from a royal building programme that was attempting to spread Catholicism throughout a 'godless' land. The small Norman church is now all but gone, smothered in centuries of expansions and extensions that have created a huge building over 61 m (200 ft) long. Some elements from the late fourteenth/early fifteenth centuries do however remain, for example the spire.

St Giles has had a highly eventful history. It was burned by the forces of Richard II (r. 1377–99) in 1385, and during the Reformation of the 1600s much of beauty was torn out to make way for Presbyterian austerity. During this period the great John Knox (1510–72) was St Giles' minister, and the church received additional walls to create multiple rooms and chapels. These changes were effectively reversed during the Restoration period in the late seventeenth century. Note that it was during the seventeenth century, under Charles I and II, that the church became a cathedral, owing to periods as an Episcopal institution (meaning it was the seat of a bishop). Yet St Giles was central to anti-Episcopal rebellion, being the place of the Jenny Geddes riot and also the site where the National Covenant (*see* p.104) was drawn up and ratified. Both the Marquis of Montrose (*see* p.113) and the Marquis of Argyll (*see* p.116) were executed outside the church, and some of Montrose's remains are interred in the church itself.

The architect William Burn (1789–1870) supervised major restoration work at St Giles in the nineteenth century, during which the traditional Victorian obsession with the Gothic crept in, and further restoration during the twentieth century was more sensitively handled. Although technically a church, St Giles retains its cathedral title in popular usage, and it stands as a visible symbol of Edinburgh's turbulent spiritual past.

David I (r. 1124–53)

Edinburgh has been physically shaped by the efforts of Scotland's many kings, and David I left his own stamp during a 19-year reign. David was born in 1050, the son of Malcolm III and Queen Margaret, and spent his early years in the English court of Henry I (r. 1100–35), becoming the Earl of Huntingdon in 1113. In 1124, however, he ascended to the throne of Scotland, and such was the power and scope of his reign that it has been subsequently referred to as the 'Davidian revolution'. Much like his mother, David was an especially pious leader, but his spirituality was backed by a politically savvy mind. David brought Norman influences into Scotland, further modernizing Scottish society.

He oversaw the settlement of much Scottish territory by Anglo-Norman lords, and completely revamped systems of government – he introduced the first system of Scottish coinage, and founded royal burghs as new administrative organizations to govern principal towns and cities. Stirling, Dunfermline, Berwick, Aberdeen, Perth and Scone became burghs under David, and were joined by Edinburgh itself. Yet David kept enough of traditional Celtic social structure to avoid evoking the ire of too many indigenous lords.

David's sincerely held religious faith produced much ecclesiastical building, including 10 new Scottish monasteries. Edinburgh received Holyrood Abbey (*see* below) and one of its oldest surviving buildings – St Margaret's Chapel (*see* p.34) atop Edinburgh Castle. David was one of Scotland's greatest kings, and visible reminders stand throughout Scotland, not just in the capital.

Holyrood Abbey

Today a ruin in the grounds of Holyrood Palace, albeit a beautiful one, Holyrood Abbey was founded in 1128. Its origins have a mystical quality to them. The story goes that in 1127 King David I was hunting in the forests around Edinburgh when he was confronted by a powerful stag. He was saved from death by goring by two local brothers, an incident that David regarded as something of a miracle. In recognition of divine salvation, David founded Holyrood Abbey the following year, its crest depicting a stag with the Christian cross between its antlers and bearing the motto *Tutum te robore reddam* – 'I will give you safety by strength'.

The legend is unlikely to be true – stories of salvation from aggressive stags abound both before and after David's reign – and it was more likely built as part of the fervour for worship of the cross sweeping across Europe in the twelfth century (David himself believed that he had a fragment of the true cross). Whatever the case, for the next 600 years Holyrood Abbey was a place not only of religious worship, but also of royal ceremony and occasion. It also suffered from its fair share of depredations – in was plundered by the Earl of Hertford during the 1540s and similar treatment was meted out by the people of Edinburgh during the Glorious Revolution of 1688. It changed Christian faiths on several occasions, and in 1691 it lost its function as the local parish church to the Kirk of the Canongate. Lapsing into decay, the Abbey was hit by a huge storm in 1768, which ripped off the roof and left it as a permanent ruin.

Royal High School

Another legacy of the reign of King David I, the Royal High School, was founded in 1128, and although its building and the location has changed several times throughout the centuries, as a school the Royal High ranks as one of the oldest in Europe.

The Royal High School's original location was in the grounds of Holyrood Abbey – the school was founded and run by Augustinian friars who had previously delivered religious and academic education from Edinburgh Castle. As a seminary the school flourished until the fourteenth century, around which time it developed into the Grammar School of the Church of Edinburgh, and was primarily focused on the education of burgess families. Another change came about during the sixteenth century, when the institution passed from church hands into those of the Edinburgh town council. This occurred in 1566, under the influence of the Scottish Reformation, and in 1590 came the school's royal charter, as James VI (r. 1567–1625) granted it the title *Schola Regia Edinensis*.

Since that time the Royal High School has occupied five different locations around Edinburgh, its last being Barton, from where it has taught since 1968. It is also now a mixed school, girls having been admitted since 1973. Space here does not allow a full list of the luminaries that have received education at the Royal High School, but they include Sir Walter Scott, Alexander Graham Bell (1847–1922) and also the comedian Ronnie Corbett (b. 1930). The school's survival throughout the centuries is sound testimony to its academic credentials.

William the Lion (r. 1165–1214)

William I of Scotland is known to posterity as William 'the Lion' on account of the red lion rampant displayed on his standard, a motif that survives to this day on the Royal Standard of Scotland. Despite the martial ferocity of his logo, William's reign included a spectacular military failure, one that resulted in the temporary transfer of Edinburgh Castle to English ownership.

William was born in *c.* 1142, son of Malcolm IV (r. 1153–65), and grew to be a strapping, ambitious young man. From his grandfather, David I, he inherited the title Earl of Northumberland in 1152, a territory that he lost in 1157 as Henry II (r. 1154–89) of England appropriated many of the Scottish border territories. This loss rankled William, and some eight years into his reign as king he led an invasion of Northumberland, hoping to take advantage of the revolt of 1173–74 against Henry's rule. The invasion was an embarrassing failure – William was defeated at the Battle of Alnwick and captured, serving out his prison time in Newcastle, Northampton and then Normandy. For Edinburgh there were also consequences. Edinburgh Castle, along with three other Scottish castles, passed into English control as ransom. William was released under the conditions of the Treaty of Falaise (1174), in which he accepted English supremacy and had to pay for the English occupation army. Henry could also decide on William's bride – William was married to Ermengarde de Beaumont, a granddaughter of King Henry I, although she came with Edinburgh Castle as her dowry.

The defeat at Alnwick must not warp our view of William's reign. He improved much about Scottish administration, including the establishment of new burghs, and he successfully crushed several rebellions from within Scottish territory. He also stands as one of the longest-reigning Scottish monarchs. He died in 1214 and was buried in Arbroath Abbey.

Alexander II (r. 1214–49)

Alexander's royal claim to fame is that it was under his reign that the first Scottish Parliament (*see* p.41) convened. It was held in Edinburgh Castle, probably in 1215. Alexander presided over Edinburgh and Scotland from 1214 to 1249. He followed in the footsteps of a long line of competent Scottish rulers, although his father, William the Lion (*see* p.39), had suffered the ignominy of defeat at the Battle of Alnwick during his attempts to claw back his territories in Northumberland. Alexander also asserted his claims over Northumberland, but with a much higher degree of success. He allied himself with the English barons who revolted against King John (r. 1199–1216) in 1215 over the establishment of the Magna Carta. Alexander literally waded into the revolt, sending military forces into England as far down as Dover and gaining the barons' approval for his claims to Northumberland, Cumberland and Westmorland. Not all went Alexander's way, however, and subsequent defeats plus French political interference meant that he lost many of his English acquisitions. In 1216 John died, and was replaced by Henry III (r. 1216–72). Between them these two monarchs brought more peace to Britain: Henry accepting Scottish independence, and Alexander subsequently rejecting Scottish expansion. These sentiments were given substance through Alexander's marriage to Henry's sister, Joan, and through the Treaty of York in 1237. For the rest of his reign Alexander focused on quashing Scottish rebellions until his death on Kerrera, an island in Oban Bay, in 1249.

The First Scottish Parliament

Being a medieval Scottish monarch was a lonely and politically complex job, especially as the Scottish kingdom took on its recognizable shape and extent during the eleventh century. In addition to the demands of court and internal Scottish disputes, the monarch also had to negotiate the legal and military minefields of relations with England and France. Little wonder, therefore, that there soon emerged the need for a more formal body of advisers to the king who could guide him on matters of state. In short, the king needed a Parliament.

Evidence for the establishment of the first Scottish Parliament is hard to pin down, although it almost certainly occurred during the reign of Alexander II (*see* p.40). The first Parliament is likely to have been convened in 1215 and was held in Edinburgh Castle, the city which to this day holds the seat of Scotland's Parliament. (It should be noted, however, that the word 'colloquium' – a medieval reference equivalent to 'Parliament' – is not seen until a document dated 1235.) Unlike today, Edinburgh's medieval Parliament was not a permanently sitting body, rather it was periodically called by the monarch to sit and weigh a particular issue. The Parliament members were a mix of religious authorities, nobility and burgh commissioners, and together these three groups became known as the 'Three Estates'. Although the Scottish Parliament was a single entity (unlike the English equivalent, which was split between the Lords and the Commons), various committees supported it by drafting legislation. So began a long road of Scottish governance from Edinburgh.

Alexander III (r. 1249-86)

Alexander III is held, and with some justice, as one of the greatest of all the Scottish kings. Under his reign, which was generally characterized by peaceful relations with England (thanks in part to Henry III's respect for Scottish independence), Scotland grew in prosperity and security, and Edinburgh thrived under Alexander's court and influence.

Alexander ascended the throne in 1249 at the age of only seven, the country led by regents until Alexander was capable of taking power for himself in 1264. Building upon the legacy of his father, Alexander II (see p.40), Alexander III focused upon expanding Scotland's trade and infrastructure. He promoted the commercial activity of the burghs, and his only military activity (traditionally a good way to strip the coffers of any nation) was his efforts to reclaim the Western Isles from the rule of Norway. In this he was successful, thereby adding to the size and power of the Scottish state. He also maintained good relations with Scottish lords and landowners, helping to foster a spirit of unity that inspires many Scottish nationalists even today.

Yet amidst all the success and achievement, there were seeds of future problems. First, all of Alexander's three children died between 1281 in 1284, leaving him without an heir. Nor was there time enough to sire a son and heir because of tragic events that occurred on 18 March 1286. He had spent the day in debate at Edinburgh Castle, but as the day gave way to a stormy evening he set off on a journey to Fife to see his wife, against recommendations by nobles and family. During the journey, Alexander was thrown from his horse and killed, bringing his reign to an abrupt end and leaving Scotland with an uncertain future.

The Great Cause

In 1291 a political situation developed that was to have not only a powerful impact on Edinburgh, but also on the whole of Scotland. The Scottish king Alexander III had died in March 1286 in a riding accident, leaving his infant granddaughter, Princess Margaret (1283–90), the Maid of Norway, as heiress to the Scottish throne. Edward I of England (r. 1272–1307) proposed a marriage between Margaret and his own son (the future Edward II), but in 1290 the Maid died, leaving Scotland in the dangerous position of having no obvious heir.

The primary claimants to the throne were John Balliol (r. 1292–96) and Robert the Bruce (r. 1306–29), all born of Alexander's daughters, with Balliol technically having the most convincing claim to the throne. As each man made his case, civil war began to look likely, so in October 1290 religious authorities in Scotland asked Edward I to intervene and solve the dispute in favour of Balliol. Edward declared himself Superior and Lord Paramount of Scotland, and gathered Scottish barons at Norham Castle in May 1291 to force their seal of approval for his new role. Once this was secured, he then announced his choice of Balliol for the Scottish throne, and on 18 November 1292 Balliol unwillingly swore his allegiance to Edward, being crowned king on 30 November. Thus was settled what became known as the 'Great Cause', but it bode ill for the future of Edinburgh and Scotland, bringing English power into the heart of the Scottish court.

John Balliol and the Events of 1292-96

Although John Balliol was Edward I's own choice for king of Scotland, the relationship between the two countries was not to end well and would lead to English armies invading the streets of Edinburgh and other Scottish towns and cities. From the outset the English king treated Balliol as an inferior – Edward's position as Lord Paramount of Scotland gave him feudal powers over Scottish territory, and Balliol effectively became Edward's vassal. Balliol was humiliated in front of his own court, and Edward also made demands that Balliol frequently present himself in London, a long and disruptive distance from Balliol's seats of power in Edinburgh and Stirling.

Resentment over Scottish subjugation quickly built amongst the Scottish nobles, and in 1295 a group of 12 such nobles organized themselves into a council at Stirling, and effectively pulled leadership of the country away from Balliol. Yet Balliol was keen to show his independent credentials, and later in the year, when Edward was distracted by military events in Wales and Gascony, he and his advisors travelled to the French court, where they arranged a mutual assistance pact with France, what became known as the 'Auld Alliance' (see p.66). This decision clearly moved Scotland onto dangerous ground – Edward had been at war with France since 1294, and would see any formal bond between the two as an effective declaration of war.

Outbreak of War 1296

John Balliol's negotiation of the Auld Alliance with France, secured by the marriage of his son, Edward Balliol (c. 1282–1364), to the niece of France's King Philip (r. 1285–1314), Jeanne de Valois, was a stinging slap in the face for England's Edward I. What he had regarded as the vassal state now became a dangerous threat north of the English border.

Edward now drew up an invasion force and headed for Scotland. He was a hard-hearted king, and not inclined to mercy. His first target was Berwick, which Edward took in fairly short order and then gave his soldiers licence to massacre its occupants, a process that took a hideous three days. The advance then continued and Edinburgh was soon a target. Edward's troops quickly moved through Edinburgh's streets and launched an attack against Edinburgh Castle. Despite the strength of its fortifications, the castle was unable to resist the English onslaught and it capitulated. Recognizing the value of the castle as a controlling point in Scotland, Edward installed a large garrison – in 1300 the total number of English troops in the castle numbered 347. Other conquests included Roxburgh and Stirling, and on 7 July 1296 Balliol finally surrendered to Edward and abdicated the throne. Edward then set about crushing the symbols of Scottish identity, smashing up the Great Seal of Scotland and moving the Stone of Destiny (*see* p.201) from Scone down to Westminster. What Scotland now needed more than anything else was a hero.

Robert the Bruce (1274–1329)

Edward I's military occupation of Scotland quickly encountered fierce resistance. One branch of the Scottish uprising was led by the great William Wallace (d. 1305), known for his impressive defeat of the English army at Falkirk in 1297. Yet another would come from Robert the Bruce. Bruce, a Scottish noble, did not have a promising start as a resistance hero. In 1296 he was actually a supporter of Edward I's invasion of Scotland against John Balliol, but an event in February 1306 changed the political landscape. Bruce met in Greyfriars church, Dumfries, to settle a rivalry with John Comyn, Balliol's nephew and a contender for the Scottish throne. Negotiations did not go well – Bruce murdered Comyn within the church, resulting in Edward branding him an outlaw. Bruce now declared himself king of Scotland, and was crowned at Scone on 27 March.

Bruce now began a vigorous guerrilla war against the English, leading to a major Scottish victory over Edward II (r. 1307–27; Edward I had died in 1307) at Bannockburn in 1314. By this time, Bruce had already released Edinburgh from the English grip, taking back the castle in a raid by his commander Sir Thomas Randolph, Earl of Moray (d. 1332; see 'Reclaiming the Castle', below). With Bannockburn, Scotland was once again back in independent Scottish hands, although Edward II refused to accept this. Nevertheless, in 1324 Bruce was accepted as the king of Scotland by the Pope and by 1327 – by which time Edward had been deposed – peace was declared between Scotland and England. Bruce died on 7 June 1329, a hero of Scottish identity.

Reclaiming the Castle

By 1313, Edinburgh Castle was in English hands. It had fallen to the English army of Edward I at the outbreak of the Scottish Wars of Independence in 1296. Edward was keen to see that this great bastion did not return to Scottish hands, so garrisoned it with nearly 350 English troops. Yet by the spring of 1313 those troops were in something of a beleaguered position. Robert the Bruce's campaign against English occupation was bearing significant fruit, including major defeats of English forces in open battle at places such as Loudoun Hill, Ayrshire, in 1307.

The task of taking Edinburgh Castle back for the Scots fell to Thomas Randolph, 1st Earl of Moray. Randolph was faced with the challenge of how to defeat the immense fortress, and the solution came from within his ranks. One of his soldiers, named William Frank, told Randolph that as a young man he had used a little-known access point to the castle to make secret visits to a woman within. Franks offered to lead a small raiding party into the castle via the same route, which was accessible only by rope ladder.

Randolph seized on the plan, and along with Frank as guide and 30 other soldiers he silently scaled the rock using a rope ladder and the night as cover for their action. Although at one point they thought they had been spotted, it proved to be false alarm, and eventually the raiding party worked its way into the castle interior. A fierce hand-to-hand battle ensued, but the English were psychologically thrown by the attack. Those of the garrison who were not killed, or who did not commit suicide by throwing themselves from the battlements, surrendered to Randolph, and the castle was once again back in Scottish hands. Bruce ordered the defences to be destroyed so that the castle could not serve as a buttress for resistance again.

A Disastrous Invasion

Following England's defeat at Bannockburn in 1314, Scottish forces made frequent raids into England, usually against poor English resistance. In 1322, however, the fortunes of Edward II seemed to take a momentary upturn. At the Battle of Boroughbridge in March, Edward defeated forces of the rebel English barons who were forging an alliance with Bruce in Scotland. Following this victory, the moment seemed right for Edward to make a concerted push back into Scotland to try to reclaim the country that he felt belonged under the English heel.

Edward gathered together a large force of cavalry and foot soldiers, critically omitting to include the large units of English archers who probably could have proved decisive in the forthcoming campaign. The advance began in August, but Bruce gave orders for his troops to employ a scorched-earth retreat, destroying food and poisoning water supplies, and so leaving nothing for the English forces to forage. As the English soldiers began to suffer from starvation, the Scottish troops made frequent guerrilla attacks and ambushes, wearing down the English numbers further.

Edinburgh was the furthest point of the English advance. By the time they reached the city the soldiers were in a desperate state, especially as the city itself had been stripped of much of its useful food. The English forces soon succumbed to reality and began their retreat back to England, but not before they had taken some measure of vengeance on Edinburgh. In an act of outright vandalism, Holyrood Abbey was destroyed and looted. The destruction served no purpose, and within five years the Abbey was back in full operation.

Treaty of Edinburgh-Northampton

Following Edward's failed invasion of Scotland in 1322, his beleaguered forces were forced back by the Scots down as far as Yorkshire. Seeing an imminent threat to his throne, Edward negotiated a truce with the

Scots in May 1323. Nevertheless, his faithfulness to the treaty was less than complete, and he allowed English privateers to attack Scottish trading vessels moving between Flanders and Scotland.

In 1327 Edward was deposed and murdered, by which time fighting had broken out again between England and Scotland. A young Edward III (r. 1327–77) occupied the throne, and his representatives began negotiations to settle the seemingly interminable conflict between the two countries. On 17 March 1328, the King's Chamber in Holyrood Abbey in Edinburgh became the location of a historic agreement. There the English formalized a treaty that gave up all English claims to political power over Scotland, leaving Robert the Bruce as the undisputed king of the nation. To give weight to the agreement, Edward III's younger sister was promised in marriage to the son of Robert the Bruce. The treaty was then ratified in Parliament at Northampton on 3 May.

The treaty of Edinburgh-Northampton marked the end of a particularly long and bloody period in Scotland's history. For the city of Edinburgh, the wars of Scottish independence had also visited its own streets, with bitter fighting to secure the castle and the unwarranted destruction of Holyrood Abbey in 1322. For the moment at least, there would be peace.

Robert's Royal Charter

The fortunes of Leith and Edinburgh would become inextricably intertwined over the centuries, leading right up to Leith's official absorption into Edinburgh in 1920 (against much opposition from the people of Leith). In the medieval period they were separate burghs, but Leith's position at the maritime access point to Edinburgh, meant that it was in Edinburgh's interest to assert some form of control.

Various royal charters were often the means by which Edinburgh exerted its influence over Leith, none more so than Robert the Bruce's charter of 28 May 1329. The charter was clear in its prescriptions:

> Robert, by the grace of God king of Scots, to all good men of his land, greeting: Know ye that we have given, granted, and to perform let, and by this our present charter confirmed, to the burgesses of our burgh of Edinburgh, our foresaid burgh of Edinburgh, together with the port of Leith, mills, and their pertinents, to have and to hold, to the said burgesses and their successors...

The charter brought with it control over Leith port, which subsequently developed rapidly under Bruce's rule, and thereby increased the levels of trade and prosperity for the city of Edinburgh. Acquisition of land around Leith would expand over the coming decades and centuries, and its burgh would gain considerably in importance, to the extent that at points in its history it was the centre of the Scottish court.

David II (r. 1329-71)

David II was another long-reigning Scottish monarch, the longevity of his rule principally accounted for his by his ascension to the throne at the age of five. The early years of his minority would prove traumatic. In 1333 the victories of the English invasion forces under Edward III and Edward Balliol forced David to flee to France and there he would remain until 1341. In 1346 he went one stage further, invading England but suffering a critical defeat at the Battle of Neville's Cross, Durham, and thereafter entering 11 years of captivity in England. He was not released until 1357, his ransom involving a commitment to allow an English prince to take the Scottish throne after David died, although this agreement was later rejected by the Scottish nobles, and David also later turned his back on it. For the rest of his rule David remained in Scotland where he proved himself, like many of his predecessors, to be an adept ruler. He controlled his state with an authoritarian hand, imposing heavy taxes (in part to pay off his ransom to the English) and controlling rebellion from wayward Scottish nobles.

David would be intimately connected with the development of Edinburgh Castle. In 1356 he implemented a major programme of defensive redevelopment, rebuilding the war-ravaged fortress in powerful stoneworks. (Note, however, that much of the building work did not commence until the 1360s because of the continuing troubles of the English.) His greatest extension to the castle was 'David's Tower', an L-shaped tower to the east of the castle that towered up 30 m (98 ft). This mighty bastion was not completed until 1371, and it was the location of David's death in the same year. Low-level ruins of his mighty tower remain to this day, although its full glory was destroyed during a siege action in the sixteenth century.

The Tolbooth

Outside the High Kirk of St Giles is a heart-shaped marker set in the cobbles of the street, known as the Heart of Midlothian. It is an attractive image, but one frequently covered in spittle by contemptuous passers-by. The reasons for its condition can be argued, but there is no doubting that it marks the former site of one of Edinburgh's most detested historical buildings, the Tolbooth.

The Tolbooth was for over 400 years an administrative centre for the city of Edinburgh. It was built in 1386 on the north-west corner of St Giles, a replacement for an earlier building that had been destroyed by the English the previous year. Over its subsequent history the Tolbooth performed a colourful array of civic roles. Up until the seventeenth century, it housed the high courts and acted as the national Parliament, but then also served as civic headquarters, council chambers, tax office and prison. It was in the latter role that the Tolbooth became infamous – it was a squalid and brutal place in which to be incarcerated. In *Traditions of Edinburgh* (1868), Robert Chambers (1802–71) quotes the lines that ran over the door of the prison chapel, which included:

A prison is a house of care,
a place where none can thrive,
a touchstone true to try a friend,
a grave for men alive.

The fear and loathing that the Tolbooth inspired may account for the spitting on the site today (although territorial football rivalries is another explanation). With the opening of the new Bridewell prison in 1817 the 'Auld Tolbooth' was torn down. But as the Heart of Midlothian indicates, its memory remains.

James I (r. 1406-37)

James I took to the throne at the tender age of 12, destined to become a politically divisive ruler. His younger years were a time of civil war and violence, during which he was forced to flee from Scotland and ended up in English captivity. By the time he was king, James was a lover of English customs and administration – he was particularly inspired by Henry V (r. 1413–22) – but he wasn't permitted to re-enter Scotland until 1424, bringing with him not only his wife, Queen Joan, but also the need to finance a large ransom, which he did by the always popular method of raising taxes.

James proved to be an efficient and disciplined ruler, albeit one with a flair for ruthlessness. He acted against the Stewart family, his long-standing rivals for power, and arrested a whole swathe of other people who might potentially threaten his supremacy. As he did so, James made more than his fair share of enemies.

James was closely connected with the city of Edinburgh, and his residence known as the King's Great Chamber was built within the castle grounds from 1434. James did not get to use the Chamber long, however. Having been politically weakened by a series of military and political defeats, on 21 February 1437 James was murdered during an attempted coup at the Friars Preachers Monastery in Perth. (The coup leader was Walter Stewart, the Earl of Atholl.) James' son, James II (r. 1437–60) stepped into his father's troubled shoes.

A Burgeoning City

The Renaissance was a period of intellectual and commercial expansion for much of Europe, and the city of Edinburgh was not excluded. Under the hands of a series of authoritarian monarchs, from James II to James IV, Edinburgh expanded in both size and prosperity, spurred on by new forms of industry and a growth in population.

Expansion in Edinburgh was fuelled by several factors. First, there was a significant increase in the volume of trade, particularly overseas trade in wool. Wool was shipped out in vast quantities from Leith harbour, its primary destinations being Flanders, France and Italy. The fact that until 1597 all goods imported into Scotland were free from excise duty also promoted a vibrant trade. With this commercial growth, the ever-increasing centralization of government in Edinburgh, the city being declared the Scottish capital by the sixteenth century, and a subsequent growth in population, it was clear that Edinburgh was set to expand.

Physical expansion had its limits. To the north the Nor'Loch prevented effective growth in that direction, so the buildings spread principally to the south. Two of Edinburgh's great streets, the Grassmarket and Cowgate (at first called Southgate), were built during the late medieval and Renaissance periods. The Grassmarket was so called because it was developed initially as a market, its valley location giving it easier access to livestock, while the Cowgate was, as its name suggests, the route by which livestock were led into the city. Yet such areas quickly became crowded and squalid, with multi-storey tenements being the only answer to the growing housing shortage. By the beginning of the seventeenth century Edinburgh Old Town was established as one of the most bustling urban centres in Britain.

James II (r. 1437–60)

Of all the places in Edinburgh, James II is most associated with Holyrood Abbey. There the king was born, crowned (making him the first Scottish king since Kenneth I not to be crowned at Scone), married and buried, although the holy association did not confer on James spiritual quietness and passivity. James was born in 1430, and following the pattern of many previous Scottish monarchs he was crowned king as a child, in 1437. An angry-looking vermilion birthmark on his face combined with his strident personality to create an unnerving appearance.

James was brought up in a poisonous atmosphere. The killers of his father, James I (*see* p.54) had been put to death, but the young James was effectively governed by members of the scheming Black Douglas family, one of the most powerful families in Scotland, who controlled the child king for their own ends. Even once James took the reins of power, the Douglases still wielded a heavy influence.

The situation could not last, and steadily the king cast off Douglas control. At the infamous 'Black Dinner' in Edinburgh Castle in November 1440, James arranged a mock trial of the 6th Earl of Douglas and his brother, summarily having them beheaded. On 22 February 1452 James personally murdered William, the 8th Earl of Douglas, in Stirling Castle, whereupon there began a period of inconclusive civil war between James and the Douglases. Only by the mid 1450s, aided by the English distraction of the War of the Roses and the shifting allegiances of the Scottish nobility, did James finally crush the Douglas estates.

James seems to have gained something of a taste for war during this period and proved to be politically and militarily belligerent for the rest of his reign. He was killed by an exploding cannon at the siege of Roxburgh in August 1460.

The City Walls

By the 1450s it was only natural that a siege mentality was developing amongst Edinburgh's court. Civil conflict within Scotland between James II and the Douglases, in addition to perennial threats from the English to the south, meant that the city appeared vulnerable to being overrun. James saw the answer in the construction of a defensive wall around much of the city. The wall would add to the natural defences already possessed by Edinburgh (the elevated position of the castle, plus surrounding marshes and lakes).

Evidence about the exact nature and extent of what became known as the 'King's Wall' is unclear, as centuries of urban development has steam-rollered much of it out of existence. Furthermore, some experts contend with the idea that it was built under James' reign at all, arguing that it was actually the English who constructed the wall some 100 years earlier during an occupation of Edinburgh. Whatever the case, the wall snaked outwards from the castle ramparts, tracked roughly parallel to what is now Johnston Terrace and High Street, then terminated at the corner of the North Loch.

The construction of the wall imposed some tight limits on urban development, resulting in the building of many high-rise structures in the city (*see* 'Medieval Manhattan', p.58). Parts of the wall still crop up during building work, the 2-m (6.6-ft) thick stonework easily standing out amongst much more fragile modern structures.

Medieval Manhattan

With the King's Wall wrapping itself around Edinburgh, the options for expanding the city's housing outwards were strictly limited. Once horizontal space was filled, there was only one way for Edinburgh's buildings to go, and that was upwards. And upwards they went in style. What developed were tenement buildings that in some cases reached 15 storeys high. Narrow passageways ran in the almost subterranean gloom between the buildings, linking streets to one another. In many ways Renaissance Edinburgh was a place of skyscrapers.

There were major social and environmental consequences to the development of Edinburgh in this way. Fire was a major hazard, there being few escape routes from such tall buildings, and many of the structures relied heavily on wood and thatch in their construction, although as the period went on more buildings were erected or converted using stone with slate, tile or lead roofs. (A Parliamentary Act of 1624 forbade the use of thatch in Edinburgh's roofing.) Sometimes the structural integrity of the buildings left a lot to be desired, with collapses being a not uncommon event, typically accompanied by a substantial loss of life. Sanitation also became a chronic problem in the overcrowded spaces, and diseases mild and serious spread with ease, especially as the density of the housing provided little in the way of ventilation. This problem would exist for centuries, leading to the Old Town being nicknamed 'Auld Reekie' (*see* p.107). What the city did have in abundance, however, was character, and this still survives in the high-rise parts of modern Edinburgh.

Mons Meg

On 14 October 1681, a huge blast reverberated across Edinburgh. The noise was heard 3.2 km (2 miles) from its source, the ramparts of Edinburgh Castle. The occasion was the birthday of the Duke of Albany and York (who later became King James VII of Scotland and II of England), and the noise itself came from a massive artillery piece, known as 'Mons Meg'.

Mons Meg is accurately defined as a bombard – a heavy cannon used to fire massive stone or iron balls against fortifications during a siege action. Its name derives from its Belgian place of origin. Meg was one of two enormous guns cast in c. 1449 and presented to King James in 1457 by Phillip the Good, Duke of Burgundy (1396–1467). The power of the gun was unnerving. It had a calibre of 56 cm (22 in) and was capable of hurling a 150 kg (330 lb) stone ball for a distance of 3.2 km (2 miles), the ball crushing almost anything that it struck. It required so much gunpowder to fire that it could only launch about eight balls a day, such was the period of time needed between each shot to allow the cannon to cool. The weapon was never really practical, as its huge weight made it a monster to transport. Nevertheless, it was used once during the siege of Norham Castle on the River Tweed in 1497. Thereafter it was sent to Edinburgh Castle for ceremonial firings. This role was actually its undoing, for the 1681 firing split the barrel. In 1754 the silent gun was taken to the Tower of London, but it returned to Edinburgh Castle in 1829.

James III (r. 1460–88)

James III underwent his coronation in 1460 at the age of only eight, his father having been blown apart by a cannon at the siege of Roxburgh. James finally took power for himself in 1468, and married Margaret of Oldenburg (1456–86), daughter of Christian I of Denmark-Norway (r. 1448–81), in 1476 at Holyrood in Edinburgh. Christian's inability to find the finance for an adequate dowry led to his pawning the Shetland and the Orkney Islands, thus expanding the Scottish kingdom when Christian defaulted on payments.

James' subsequent reign was somewhat less than successful. He was financially profligate and created an Edinburgh court of sycophants through his easy bestowal of honours and favours. He also made plenty of enemies. James alienated both of his brothers, suspecting them as rivals to his throne – Alexander, Duke of Albany (c. 1454–85), fled to France and John, Earl of Mar (c. 1456–c. 1479), died in custody after being imprisoned. Yet Albany returned in 1482 with an English army in tow, and James was overthrown and imprisoned in Edinburgh Castle. Although James clawed back power through the assistance of the Scottish nobility, he eventually lost their support as well, and that of his own family. (He was said to have poisoned his queen, who died in July 1486.) He was eventually defeated and killed by his own son's army at the Battle of Sauchieburn in June 1488.

While he lived in Edinburgh, James had a major impact on the city. He declared Edinburgh as the capital of Scotland, and his affection for the people of the city lead to his granting the 'Golden Charter', which gave city magistrates more local law-making powers. He also conferred the 'Blue Blanket' banner to the city's trades people, created by the queen and her attendants and established as a rallying point for trade militancy. Yet ultimately James was not a popular king, and so couldn't survive long in power.

James IV (r. 1488–1513)

James IV's coronation took place under a dark cloud – the killing of his own father. Throughout his life James would remain troubled by this act – he wore a physically draining iron belt around his waist as penance. Nevertheless, James would go on to become one of Scotland's most popular monarchs, and would pull Edinburgh and the rest of Scotland firmly into the Renaissance.

James was crowned king in 1488, but did not take over power effectively until 1495. Once he did, however, he threw himself into his duties with fervour and ambition. Readjusting his sources of income raised royal revenue from £13,000 p.a. to £40,000 p.a. by the end of his reign, and he spent much of this on creating a glittering court in Edinburgh, the official seat of his power. He oversaw the renovation of the castle, including the building of the spectacular Great Hall, completed in 1511. (He also transformed the castle into one of Britain's premier gun foundries.) In architectural terms, however, James is most known for the building of Holyrood Palace, a venue that had added a real sparkle to royal life. Alongside building projects, James invested heavily in arts and science. He established the first printing press in Scotland in 1508, and in 1506 the Royal College of Surgeons in Edinburgh was established through James' royal charter. He also founded a major Scottish navy, constructing capacious royal dockyards at Leith and Newhaven. Yet James' fire would be extinguished in war. His involvement on the French side against Henry VIII (r.1509–47) in 1513 led to his death at the Battle of Flodden (*see* p.67), where Scotland lost a great leader.

Palace of Holyroodhouse

Holyrood Palace began its life as a guest-house development of Holyrood Abbey, its construction beginning in 1498. Today it stands as Queen Elizabeth II's official residence in Scotland, and its long-standing royal connections are often overlooked in favour of Edinburgh Castle's bold history. Yet by the time James IV had transformed the building into a fully functioning royal palace by the early years of the sixteenth century, Holyrood Palace was already on its way to becoming a place steeped in royal intrigue and events.

James IV shared the palace with his wife Margaret Tudor, while Bonnie Prince Charlie (1720–88) brought sparkle and glamour to the palace in 1745 by hosting extravagant balls in the Picture Gallery. Less pleasant was the tenure of Mary, Queen of Scots (r. 1542–67), in which the palace witnessed the hideous murder of a private secretary and confidant David Rizzio (c. 1533–66); see 'The Murder of David Rizzio', p.120).

The palace also attracted royal residents from overseas. One of the most distinguished of these was the man who would become Charles X of France (r. 1824–30), who as the Comte d'Artois had fled France during the Revolution of 1789. He and his entourage eventually took up residence in Holyrood for 19 years. Furthermore, in 1830 he was forced to abdicate from the French monarchy and once again returned to Holyrood.

Since then the palace has been home to numerous civic events, political gatherings (such as a reading of the Parliamentary Reform Bill of 1832) and military parades (the palace has its own large parade ground), although it is also host to more informal events during the Edinburgh Festival. Because it is an official residence of the queen, access to tourists is limited, although enough historically fascinating parts of building are open to the public to make it worth a visit.

Developments in Trade

The Renaissance period in Edinburgh and the growth of the Old Town (*see* 'A Burgeoning City', p.55) was accompanied by an equal expansion in the city's trade life. In terms of internal business, the growth of the Old Town and the development of Cowgate and the Grassmarket gave the city bustle and lively commerce. Livestock, foodstuffs and other consumer goods were traded in the markets, while along the Royal Mile grew the service industries that attended the royal court, including jewellers, lawyers and cloth merchants. Yet in commercial terms it was the development of overseas trade that had the most profound impact on the vitality of Edinburgh. Leith acted as a gateway to Europe for maritime trade, and even as early as the fourteenth century it was conducting trade with Scandinavia and the Low Countries.

By the fifteenth and sixteenth centuries a principal outward export was wool, the main destinations for this material being France, Italy and Flanders, but other commodities included grain, salt and cattle hides. With an absence of import duties until the end of the sixteenth century, imports also came flooding in from the Continent. From France came fine drinks such as wine and cognac (the Auld Alliance gave Scottish wine merchants first pick of the finest Bordeaux wines); pottery, artworks, silks and carpets from the Low Countries; Spanish oranges could be bought in the Grassmarket; and primary goods such as timber and iron were imported from Scandinavia. The net result of all this commercial activity was the development of a massive industrial infrastructure, particularly in terms of mills, warehouses and dock facilities, and an outward-looking mentality amongst the Edinburgh people that survives to this day.

A Royal Wedding

All royal weddings are magisterial events, but few more so than the lavish ceremony given by James IV for his bride, Margaret Tudor (the sister of King Henry VIII of England) in 1503. The wedding was important politically as well as personally. The marriage alliance between England and Scotland seemed to augur the end of a long period of war and enmity, brought to a close by the Treaty of Perpetual Peace of 1502 and secured with the marriage. (Ironically, the Perpetual Peace was not to last long.) For James, however, the marriage was also an opportunity to indulge his love of theatrical court life, hence he would spend the equivalent of £500,000 putting on a display for his queen and guests.

The location of the marriage festival was the Palace of Holyroodhouse, but James first treated the fourteen-year-old bride to a day or so of wooing at her reception at Newbattle, attended by manly displays of horsemanship, and romancing on the lute and clavichord. On the day of the wedding, the queen, clad in a sumptuous dress that would cost £100,000 today, was met by the king on horseback as she travelled to Edinburgh, and the theatre began in earnest. Massed ranks of knights were gathered, and there was a brief show representing one such knight rescuing a distressed damsel. The royal couple kissed equally royal relics in a solemn ceremony outside Greyfriars Kirk. The marriage itself took place on 8 August, followed by a fifteen-course dinner for all guests, then several days of tournaments and celebrations commenced. It was all very grand, and a promising start to the new Anglo-Scottish alliance. Ten years later James would be dead on the battlefield of Flodden, slain by the English.

The Auld Alliance

Much of the context for Scotland's many conflicts between the thirteenth century and the sixteenth century lies in the Auld Alliance between Scotland and France. By the later years of the thirteenth century, both countries shared a common problem – England. English expansionism needed to be curtailed, and a Franco-Scottish alliance signed in 1295 in Paris seemed to provide a solution. The treaty bound the two countries together in a mutual defence pact, and gave England the severe military headache of war on two widely separated fronts should it attack one of the treaty nations.

Thereafter, the Auld Alliance held until 1560, with commitments being renewed on a regular basis – James IV himself renewed the alliance in 1491. In a useful reciprocal arrangement, Scotland would launch an attack over the Tweed into northern England if France were attacked, while France would launch assaults against the English Channel ports if Scotland were threatened. The arrangement bore real military fruit. Scotland supplied France with thousands of mercenaries, who helped secure important victories over the English on French battlefields and won for Scottish nobles titles to French lands. English forces struggled to divert troops northwards to a rebellious Scotland when fighting against France. The Auld Alliance also brought commercial benefits to Scotland – the finest French wines were shipped into Leith to the appropriately named Wine Quay, the Edinburgh winesellers having first choice of the best wines while the English equivalents drank inferior products.

The Auld Alliance survived, but was severely shaken by the Scottish defeat at Flodden (*see* p.67) in 1513. It finally came to an end in the Reformation as England switched to Protestantism, and Scotland underwent its own revolution in 1558–60.

Battle of Flodden

Just 10 years after James IV married Henry VIII's sister, Margaret Tudor, in a spectacular ceremony in Edinburgh, the possibility of a meaningful Anglo-Scottish alliance came crashing down on the battlefield at Flodden in September 1513. The background to the battle was Henry's campaign in France against Louis XII (r. 1498–1515), a war that for Scotland invoked the terms of mutual Franco-Scottish protection embodied in the Auld Alliance. With Henry's horns thoroughly locked in France, James was confident of victory, especially as he assembled an enormous army of 30,000 men and took them into Northumberland on 22 August. The army was also supported by 17 large artillery pieces from Edinburgh, including the Mons Meg (*see* p.59) bombard, and in total 400 oxen were needed to pull the artillery train.

At first the Scottish campaign went well. In short order James' forces managed to take four major English fortresses – Norham, Etal, Wark and Ford – aided by their wall-battering artillery, but suffered heavy casualties in the actions and became demoralized under the effects of poor weather. Furthermore, by this time the English forces of Lord Surrey (26,000 men) were heading north from Newcastle. The two forces finally engaged in battle on Branxton Hill, near Flodden, on 9 September.

There began a battle of horrible, hacking violence. Although the two sides were roughly equivalent in numbers, Surrey had positioned his forces well enough to unseat James from Flodden Hill, his chosen defensive position, and in battle the Scottish pikemen were slain in huge numbers by English archers and lighter, more manoeuvrable artillery. Then James himself was killed, along with nine of his nobles, and the Scottish army began to collapse. Edinburgh and Scotland had lost yet another monarch.

Cleaning the Causeway

Edinburgh's streets have witnessed many bloody brawls over the centuries, although few so organized as an incident that occurred in April 1520, known to posterity as 'Cleaning [or 'Cleansing'] the Causeway'.

The context of the incident was Scotland's various political conflicts of the sixteenth century. These expressed themselves on the streets of Edinburgh through gangs of scrappers allied to various nobles vying for power within the city. On 30 April 1520, one such storm was gathering. At this time there were two particular clans fighting for influence over and access to the monarch James V (r. 1513–42). The first was the Clan Hamilton, led by James Hamilton, 1st Earl of Arran (c. 1475–1529), who was also the city's Lord Provost. His principal rival was the Clan Douglas, headed by Archibald Douglas, 6th Earl of Angus (1490–1557). In April 1520 the Hamiltons ventured into town in force, led by Arran himself and his brother Sir Patrick Hamilton and including Sir James Hamilton of Finnart (the Earl's bastard son) and Douglas of Bethune, the belligerent archbishop of Glasgow. Feeling threatened by the Douglases, they intended to arrest Archibald Douglas, who responded by gathering his own war party and meeting the Hamiltons head on for a street battle.

The fight took place on High Street, the Hamiltons principally armed with swords, the Douglases with spears. The Douglases also had much backing from the local population, Arran being an unpopular provost, and the Hamilton party was overwhelmed in a horrifying fight that cost

250 lives, including that of Patrick Hamilton. Arran himself fled from the scene on a hastily requisitioned coal horse.

Mary, Queen of Scots (r. 1542-67)

M ary, Queen of Scots presided over what was not only a particularly troubled time for Scotland, but also a time of bloodshed and destruction for Edinburgh. As so often in Scottish history, the problem lay to the south in England. James V was on the throne of Scotland, while in England King Henry VIII looked on Scotland as a potential acquisition. His opportunity came even as James lay on his deathbed in 1542. On 8 December James' wife, Mary of Guise (1515–60), gave birth to a baby girl who was named Mary. The fact did not please James, who reportedly said 'Woe is me. My dynasty came with a lass. It will go with a lass.' Within one week James was dead and Mary was crowned an infant queen.

Now was Henry's chance. He attempted to force a union of marriage between his son Edward and Mary, but his efforts became increasingly militaristic and the regents of Scotland began to resist (*see* The 'Rough Wooing', p.72). Instead, the regents concluded a treaty with France – Henry's great enemy – to where Mary was sent in 1548. Her journey to France was not only for her own protection, there were also plans that she would marry France's dauphin. Mary was to be away from her beloved Scotland from 1548 to 1561, and married the dauphin in 1558. Yet her future lay not in France but in Scotland, and once more she would be intimately tied to the city of Edinburgh.

Court of Session

Even today Edinburgh is known for being a respected centre of legal education and practice. One of the reasons for this status was the establishment of the Court of Session during the first half of the sixteenth century. The court was founded in 1532 by James V, who wanted a permanent and authoritative legal body to oversee cases of royal and social importance, and to act as a form of appeal court. The recommendation to create such a body may have come from the Pope, and the Court was closely modelled on the Parlement of Paris. The effect of centralizing the Court meant that Edinburgh became a magnet for those wanting to practice law, or those wanting to be defended by it, and it was also a catalyst for the founding of numerous law practices throughout the city.

Also called the Court of Justice, the Court of Session consisted of 15 members in total, no doubt judiciously selected to be politically useful. At first the Court was dominated by clerical figures, but this changed following the Reformation when more figures from outside the church were brought in to sit on the Court. The Court survived the later Act of Union intact and in fact grew steadily in terms of its number of justices and in its influence. Today the Court of Session stands as Scotland's 'supreme civil court' (in its own words), led by a Lord President with a Lord Justice Clerk as second-in-command. The justices themselves are titled either 'Lord' or 'Lady', and they preside over a wide range of civil and commercial cases.

The 'Rough Wooing'

The 'rough wooing' was to be very rough indeed. In December 1543 the regents of Scotland had rejected Henry VIII's marriage plans for his son Edward and the infant Scottish queen, Mary, preferring instead to rest upon the Auld Alliance with France. Henry decided that this was unacceptable and opted for military action in an attempt to persuade the Scottish court to decide otherwise. In 1544 Henry sent his Lord Hertford north with a large army intent on teaching the Scots a lesson and forcing a change of heart. Henry's instructions for Edinburgh were particularly ruthless: 'Put all to fire and sword. Steal everything you can from Edinburgh, then burn it and knock it down. This will always remind the Scots of their punishment for being disloyal. Do what you can to knock down the castle and burn the Palace of Holyroodhouse. Ruin as many villages around Edinburgh as you can. Destroy Leith!'

The invading English forces quickly wrapped themselves around the city, and despite appeals for clemency from the city's authorities the English set out on a campaign of destruction. Over three days the troops destroyed almost everything they could find, including Holyroodhouse, most of the Old Town and much of Leith. So many fires were started that the English were even pushed out of the city. It was a terrible act, and more violence would characterize the rough wooing until 1548, although Henry would not get his way. Mary was spirited away to France and in April 1558 she was married to the dauphin.

John Knox (c. 1510-72)

John Knox stands as one of Edinburgh's great religious leaders of the Reformation, and represents the cornerstone on which the Presbyterian church was founded. Born c. 1510, probably in Haddington in East Lothian, Knox was educated by the Scottish church and at St Andrews and Glasgow universities before going on to employment as a tutor, then a Catholic priest. It is ironic that a Catholic would become a seminal figure in the history of Protestantism. Knox converted to the Protestant faith in 1545, likely on account of his friendship with George Wishart (c. 1513–46), a religious radical who preached for the Reformation of the church in Scotland.

Knox was walking on dangerous ground. Wishart was burnt at the stake for heresy in March 1546 (Knox had actually spent time acting as Wishart's sword-wielding bodyguard), and following French military intercession into Scottish affairs Knox found himself imprisoned on a French galley ship. Once released in 1549, he travelled widely in Europe, eventually meeting the great reformer, John Calvin, in Geneva. With the Reformation and the establishment of Protestantism in Britain, Knox returned to Scotland, whipping up crowds with his sermons and fostering riots against the Catholic church. He became minister of St Giles Kirk in Edinburgh, one of many spiritual luminaries to grace the church. There he drew up the doctrines and constitution of Presbyterianism, and was the fervent spiritual voice of the Scottish Reformation. Knox was also a central figure in the Scottish government from 1560.

Knox died in 1572, but left a legacy of faith and controversy. Throughout his life he was known as a quite brilliant preacher of extremely sharp mind and violent passions. His views sit ill at ease with today's society – his most famous pamphlet was entitled 'The First Blast of the Trumpet Against the Monstrous Regiment of Women' (1558) and was aimed at Mary Tudor and Mary of Guise – but there is no doubting the colour he brings to Edinburgh's religious history.

The Scottish Reformation

The Scottish Reformation changed everything for Edinburgh and Scotland. During the sixteenth century, the Reformist ideas of Luther began to penetrate Scottish society, causing deep divisions within a highly devout society. In the 1530s James V began to toy with the ideas of Protestantism in his primarily Catholic country, but he died in 1542 and left Scotland mired in conflict between France and England over who would marry his heir, Mary, Queen of Scots. Mary fled from the 'rough wooing' (see p.72) to Paris where she married Francois, the dauphin, and Scotland remained in Catholic hands under James' widow, Mary of Guise (1515–60).

There was some Protestant resistance, however, from the likes of great theologians and preachers such as George Wishart and John Knox (*see* p.73), which the Catholic authorities managed to control (Wishart was executed and Knox was exiled). The Franco-Scottish marriage contract seemed to give Scotland a firmly Catholic destiny, and Mary Tudor's establishment of Catholicism in England seemed to give that view surety. Yet in 1558 the Protestant Elizabeth I took the English throne, and powerful Protestant Scottish nobles, known collectively as the Lords of the Congregation, began a programme of destruction that targeted Romanist buildings, especially those in Edinburgh. In 1560, their aims were boosted by the death of Mary of Guise. They gained ascendancy, taking over the government and declaring a ban on Catholicism. Protestantism seemed to have triumphed, but it had yet to reckon with the return of Mary in 1561.

Treaty of Edinburgh

The Treaty of Edinburgh transformed Scotland's international relations, as it brought to a formal end the Auld Alliance that had been Scotland's bulwark against English expansionism for several hundred years. It also had dramatic implications for Edinburgh, removing the city from the shadow of French siege forces at Leith.

By 1559 Scotland was locked in the battle for the Reformation, with the reformist Lords of the Congregation on the side of Protestantism versus the Catholic governance of Mary of Guise, the mother and regent of Mary, Queen of Scots. British military assistance from Queen Elizabeth I (r. 1558–1603) was closing around Edinburgh, so the French – fearful that they might be about to lose Scotland to Protestantism – sent a large garrison to Leith, fortifying the town for a possible defence. Many Scottish people feared English attempts at domination had now been replaced by those of the French, but Mary of Guise resisted demands that her countrymen go home. Indeed, Mary now retreated into the Leith defences for her own safety, while Edinburgh was led by its governor.

Several attacks on Leith by the Lords of the Congregation led to nothing, but matters turned against the French with the Treaty of Berwick in February 1560, in which Elizabeth promised military assistance to eject the French and establish a Protestant nation. Leith was blockaded and bombarded by the English, but the French held on stubbornly. Yet fortune stepped in with the death of Mary of Guise, and Elizabeth switched to diplomatic tactics. By the Treaty of Edinburgh, agreed on 6 July, the French pulled their troops out of Scotland and effectively out of Scottish affairs for good.

Queen Mary's Return

In 1561, shockwaves ran through Edinburgh, emanating out from Leith harbour – Mary, Queen of Scots had returned. Although Scotland had been ruled by regents during her absence in France, the Scottish Reformation had negated much of Catholic Mary's authority. Leading Protestants such as John Knox prepared for a potentially violent showdown. However, although Mary resisted some Protestant measures, such as the abolition of the Catholic Mass – she negotiated for the practice of a private mass, to be held in Holyrood Abbey – she generally left religion to its own devices, and gave room and even money to the fledgling kirk. She also handled Edinburgh, the seat of her power, reasonably well. She gave permission for the construction of the hospital of the poor at Blackfriars and also for a school at Greyfriars.

Many of the former Lords of the Congregation accepted the air of compromise, a fact that infuriated vocal Protestant radicals such as John Knox, who wanted all traces of Catholicism extirpated from Scottish life. He personally led a riotous mob down to Holyrood, fully intent on disrupting Mary's private mass. However, James Stewart, the Earl of Moray (c. 1531–70; Mary's brother-in-law and a former Protestant comrade of Knox) barred his entrance to Holyrood, and Knox was forced to retreat and thereafter resided more on the political sidelines.

It was Mary's personal life that was more the cause of her undoing. The murder of her second husband, Lord Darnley (1545–67), in Edinburgh and her subsequent controversial relationship with James Hepburn, the Earl of Bothwell (c. 1534–78), alienated her from the Scottish nobility and she was removed from office by a coup that eventually forced her abdication in 1567. Twenty more troubled years lay ahead for Queen Mary, until her execution for treason in 1587 at Fotheringhay Castle.

Edinburgh's Witches

The small cast-iron wall fountain set in a wall at the entrance to Castle Esplanade is easy to miss, yet once understood harks back to one of Edinburgh's darkest episodes. At this site 300 'witches' were burnt at the stake, generally after they had undergone lengthy periods of horrific torture. During the fifteenth and sixteenth centuries, Edinburgh was in fact one of Europe's most energetic centres for witch killing. In total some 4,000 women were put to death between 1590 and 1722, although most of the executions took place before the 1700s. The catalyst for such horror was principally a royal incident in 1590. King James VI of Scotland was on a ship off the coast, destined to meet Anne of Denmark, his future queen, when a fearsome storm blew up that nearly sank the ship. This natural occurrence was blamed on a coven of witches – who naturally confessed to their crimes under the most abject torture – and so began the bloody persecution of anyone suspected of connections with devilish rites. James himself noted that 'There is a fearful number of these detestable slaves of the devil at this time in this country', and with royal licence in place the vaguest suspicions of witchcraft could have terrible consequences. Mary, Queen of Scots' Witchcraft Act gave witchcraft the same status as heresy, meaning that Edinburgh soon came alive with the sound of execution pyres. Moreover, from the early 1600s special 'witchfinders' were appointed to root out witchcraft, and they more than justified their salary. Although the last Edinburgh witch execution was in 1722, the witchcraft statute remained on the books until the twentieth century.

The Murder of David Rizzio

If ever there was a man in the wrong place at the wrong time it was David Rizzio. Born in 1533 in Turin, Rizzio was an Italian musician and scholar whose involvement with the Court of Savoy led to diplomatic contact with Mary, Queen of Scots. Rizzio's relationship with Mary became more informal and more personal, and eventually he was employed as the queen's private secretary and confidant. The relationship may have been innocent, but that is not how many scheming courtiers saw it. Rizzio was Catholic, as was Mary, and many believed that the two were collaborating in an attempt to impose Catholicism throughout Scotland. Some felt that he was a spy for the pope.

In 1565, Mary was married to Lord Darnley (*see* 'The Murder of Lord Darnley', p.79), but the marriage was a bitter one, full of mistrust and suspicion. On his part, Darnley was jealous of the close relationship between Rizzio and Mary, and this jealousy was fostered by some of his associates. Rumours even passed around that the baby Mary was carrying by the end of 1566 (the future James VI) was actually Rizzio's, not Darnley's. Darnley had had enough. With a group of fellow plotters he burst into a dining room in the Palace of Holyroodhouse where Mary (six months pregnant) and Rizzio were dining. Rizzio was dragged from the room and stabbed 57 times to his death. It is unlikely that he was anything more to Mary than just a listening ear.

The Murder of Lord Darnley

Henry Stuart – better known to history as Lord Darnley – was born in 1545, the eldest son of Matthew Stewart, Earl of Lennox and Lady Margaret Douglas. As the great-grandson of Henry VII, and with his future in the hands of a manipulative mother, his destiny was entwined with Mary, Queen of Scots. When in his late teens, Darnley met Mary during his travels in Scotland, and the two gradually became close. On 29 July 1565 they were finally married, the ceremony taking place in the Palace of Holyroodhouse in Edinburgh. Note, however, that there were many people who did not have high opinions of Darnley. People who publicly declared themselves against the marriage included Queen Elizabeth I, James Stewart, 1st Earl of Moray (and Mary's half-brother) and the preacher John Knox.

Against such powerful opposition the future of the marriage did not bode well. Furthermore, by 1565 Darnley was becoming twisted by the desire to be king rather than consort, and his part in the murder of Mary's confidant Rizzio (*see* p.78) in 1566 showed a developing violent streak. This was effectively the beginning of attempted coup against Mary, but Mary skillfully turned Darnley against the plotters and she escaped to the safety of James Hepburn, 4th Earl of Bothwell. In February 1567 Darnley was lodging in Provost House, near Kirk O' Field church in Edinburgh, when the building disintegrated in a huge explosion. The blast did not kill Darnley immediately, but he was strangled while escaping from the ruins. Subsequent historical evidence indicates that Bothwell was behind the murder, with Mary's consent, another death within a bloody reign.

James VI (r. 1567–1625)

James VI was essentially the last true king of Scotland. From 1603, when he also took the title of King of England, the status of Edinburgh as the location of a royal court changed for good (*see* 'The Union of Crowns', p.91).

James was born of the most controversial stock – his mother was Mary, Queen of Scots and his father was the late (murdered) Lord Darnley. He entered the world in the south-east corner of the palace in Edinburgh Castle in 1566, the room being just off the Queen's bedchamber. There would be no security for the infant prince, as within 13 months Mary had been forced to abdicate and James was crowned king. Although James was surrounded by manipulative nobles in the Edinburgh court during his upbringing (one of the four regents was Mary's half-brother James Stewart), he nonetheless managed to reach maturity with a wise head on young shoulders. He was a cultured and intelligent man, but also one with ambition and a touch of ruthlessness – he made nothing more than a formal protest concerning his mother's later execution, being intent on eventually taking over the English crown from Elizabeth I. (James had made a treaty with Elizabeth that guaranteed his succession on her death.) He also needed his toughness to face down the Presbyterian kirk. James was Episcopal in leaning, believing in the necessity of bishops to rule effectively. This brought him into direct conflict with the Presbyterians, who saw the bishops as an erosion of their authority (although James was himself a Protestant).

In 1596 in St Giles Kirk, a meeting between the opposing sides turned violent, and James was forced to flee and hide in the Tolbooth. Throughout his reign James managed to inject moderation into religion, steering away from extremism. Just before he left for London in 1603, he gave an address in St Giles and reassured Edinburgh and Scotland that he would still work for their interests and financial wellbeing. He would not see the city of his birth again until 1617.

The Black Death

Medieval Edinburgh was acutely vulnerable to epidemics. The city was overcrowded, sanitary conditions were poor and poverty was severe (resulting in depressed immune systems amongst much of the population) and, worse still, Edinburgh had its very own port at Leith. This factor was to be critical in the periodic bouts of plague, or Black Death, that swept across the city from the fourteenth to the seventeenth century.

Even by the fourteenth century, Edinburgh was conducting significant maritime trade with Europe, trade that brought prosperity and vitality. Unfortunately, it also helped to bring something far less welcome. A plague had been sweeping across mainland Europe from Asia, killing millions of people in its march, and from around 1350 it entered Leith. The impact was immediate – the disease killed its victims in about three to four days from infection, and population levels were decimated. In Leith, the Preceptory of St Anthony went from being a thriving community of warrior monks to just two forlorn individuals. The disease pushed outwards from Leith into Edinburgh city itself, and there was a particularly devastating outbreak in the 1560s. Mass graves were dug throughout the city. Records from 1568 show that a huge pit was dug in Greyfriars kirkyard, but others sprang up and still yield grim archaeological discoveries to this day. Interestingly, recent tests on some of Edinburgh's pits found anthrax spores mixed in with the plague, a hideous combination. Edinburgh survived repeated plague outbreaks over the coming centuries (population reductions brought some improvements, such as more food being available), but it wouldn't be free of the curse for several hundred years. (*See also* 'The Great Plague of 1645', p.170.)

Sir William Kirkaldy of Grange (1520-73)

Sir William Kirkaldy of Grange was yet another of Edinburgh's prominent citizens who came to a sticky end in the sixteenth century. Born in 1520, the son of Sir James Kirkaldy, William grew to be an influential politician and a leading light behind the Scottish Reformation. In this context William was involved in the murder of Cardinal Beaton (1494–1546) in 1546, the cardinal being a central pillar of the Franco-Scottish alliance and an opponent of Reformist ideas. In 1547 William became a prisoner of the French in Normandy, but managed to escape in 1550 and returned to Scotland in 1557. He found himself implicated, rightly or wrongly, in several other murders, but he achieved even greater notoriety in 1567 when Mary, Queen of Scots surrendered herself to him after the Battle of Carberry Hill – he took her to Edinburgh, where she lodged in the chief magistrate's house at the Black Turnpike.

In 1570 William was made governor of Edinburgh Castle, which he held in Mary's name as religious and royal conflict tore through England and Scotland. William committed himself to holding the castle until Mary, imprisoned on the orders of Elizabeth I, could bring up an army from England. Ultimately, William held the castle against the siege for some two years, although his orders to bombard parts of surrounding Edinburgh earned him few admirers amongst the town's population (*see* 'The Lang Siege', p.84). He was finally forced to surrender the castle in May 1573, and on 30 May he was hanged in Edinburgh.

The Lang Siege

The Lang Siege of Edinburgh Castle is not an inaccurate description of events that occured from 1571 to 1573. Inside the castle during this period were the forces of Sir William Kirkaldy of Grange (*see* p.83), a noble ally to Mary, Queen of Scots. Mary had fled to England following her defeat at the Battle of Langside in 1568, whereupon she was imprisoned by Elizabeth I. Ruling Scotland at this time from Edinburgh was James Douglas, 4th Earl of Morton (1525–81), who was acting as one of the four regents during the minority of James VI. Morton was intent on reclaiming Edinburgh Castle from Kirkaldy and requested support from Elizabeth I to help in this task. His request was fulfilled in 1571 – Queen Elizabeth sent 1,000 footsoldiers and 300 cavalry up to Scotland to add to the siege forces now locking themselves around the castle.

Even with these additional forces, Kirkaldy seemed quite capable of holding out. The beginning of the end, however, came in the spring of 1573. Thirty heavy cannon were brought up from Berwick Castle to join the siege forces, and on 16 May they all opened fire in unison. Although the defenders replied in turn with their own cannon, during a week's fighting Edinburgh's defences were steadily battered down. On 23 May, David's Tower collapsed, and this cut off one of the main water supplies running into the castle. Five days later the besieging forces captured or poisoned all of the castle's remaining wells, and on 28 May Kirkaldy began to talk peace. The next day, a force of only 100 soldiers plus wives and children marched out of the castle in surrender, still defiantly waving banners. William Kirkaldy, however, was hanged for treason two days later.

James Douglas, 4th Earl of Morton
(1525-81)

James Douglas's life is deeply entwined with that of Mary, Queen of Scots, so it is no surprise that his life ended on the guillotine in Edinburgh on 2 June 1581. Power came quickly to Morton. In Edinburgh he became Lord Chancellor of Scotland in 1563, but his official role was overshadowed by court violence and intrigues. Morton allied himself against the Catholicism of Mary, Queen of Scots (*see* p.70), and was personally involved with the murder of David Rizzio. Following the killing, Morton fled to England, but a royal pardon allowed him to return to Scotland in 1567. Morton would face Mary far more openly on 15 June, when he was amongst the leadership of forces that defeated her at Carberry Hill. In the subsequent conference between the rebels and the queen, Morton helped persuade Mary to abdicate in favour of James VI (execution was her only other alternative).

Mary later escaped from her subsequent captivity, and once more she met Morton in battle at Langside on 13 May 1568. She was again defeated, and thereafter the young James VI 'ruled' Scotland under the auspices of four regents, of whom Morton was the fourth. Morton helped crush Mary's allies in Scotland at the Lang Siege, but his past deeds caught up with him. Morton was implicated in the earlier murder of Mary's husband, Lord Darnley, for which he was finally arrested in 1780, and on 2 June 1581 he was executed. His head was displayed outside the Tolbooth in Edinburgh for 18 months, until it was finally buried alongside his body in Greyfriars kirkyard.

University of Edinburgh

The University of Edinburgh, now over 400 years old, was founded by the Royal Charter of James VI in 1582. Despite its royal beginnings, however, it was very much an institution of the people. It was funded by the town council, placing the 'Tounis College' (as it was originally called) at the centre of Edinburgh's administrative and civic life.

Rather than having a central location, the College's buildings were scattered over a wide area, often in unsanitary parts of the city. An attempted change in location came in the eighteenth century. In 1798

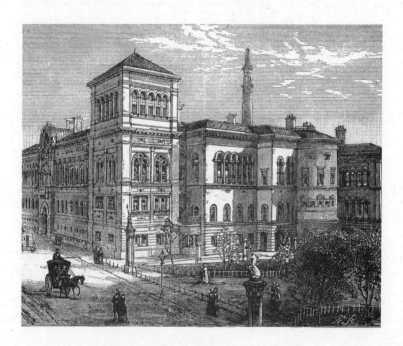

the foundation stone of what is today called the Old College was laid. Located just off South Bridge, the Old College was designed by Robert Adam (1728–92; himself an Edinburgh alumnus), but construction ground to a halt under financial pressure. Nevertheless, the university was still producing talented academics, and it had a specialism in medical studies (sometimes with grisly results – *see* 'The Burke and Hare Murders', p.179). A new medical school was built in 1875, and the Old College was finally completed in the 1820s by the architect William Playfair (Adam had died by this time).

The Old College quickly reached its capacity, and since then the university has continued its spread throughout the city at various locations, including

the New College of 1846 (home to the School of Divinity) – another Playfair design – the University Library building in George Square, and the modern King's Buildings near Blackford Hill. The list of alumni that have emerged from these buildings is prestigious and includes David Hume (1711–76), Robert Louis Stevenson (1850–94), Arthur Conan Doyle (1859–1930) and current leading figures such as Robin Cook, Stella Rimington and Ian Rankin.

Robert Rollock (1555-99)

Robert Rollock has gone down in Edinburgh history as the first principal of the University of Edinburgh. Born in 1555 he was educated in Stirling, near his birthplace, and received his university education at St Andrews. Such was his acumen that Rollock subsequently became professor of philosophy at his alma mater, yet in 1583 he was appointed as the regent of Edinburgh's college, probably as a politically safe pair of hands at a time of frequent religious upheaval. The college transformed into the University of Edinburgh, and Rollock took the title of principal in 1586 on a salary of £40 per annum. Such a salary was actually poor when compared to many other professional positions, such as the minister of a parish. Nor was his position a sinecure – he spent long hours lecturing on philosophy and later also became the university's professor of theology, although his responsibilities were nothing compared to the prolonged teaching duties of the staff beneath him, who were paid only a third of what Rollock received. Rollock was a prolific writer, and was particularly known for his works of biblical exposition, including commentaries on the books of Ephesians (1590), Thessalonians (1598), Psalms (1598) and

Galatians (1602). Known for being a moderate and calming presence in an age of religious stridency, Rollock also preached every Sunday at East Kirk and held the position of moderator of the General Assembly in 1587. Other church positions were later held at Upper Tolbooth and Greyfriars in Edinburgh. After a lifetime of spiritual service, Rollock died in Edinburgh on 8 February 1599.

A Spanish Threat

In 1588 the people of Edinburgh were steadily recovering from an horrific outbreak of plague that had killed thousands of its citizens. The plague had partly entered the city from the sea (via foreign trade), but in 1588 a new threat appeared from across the oceans – the Spanish Armada. On the orders of Catholic Philip II (1556–98) 130 ships carrying 130,000 men sailed from Lisbon in July, intent on subjugating Britain and its Protestant queen, Elizabeth I. The causes of Philip's aggression were manifold, and included Elizabeth's refusal to marry him, English piracy on Spanish ships, a Protestant revolt in The Netherlands and the execution of Mary, Queen of Scots (see p.70). His plan was for the fleet to dominate the Channel and support an invasion force from The Netherlands under the Duke of Parma.

The plan went horribly awry from the start. The British were alerted as the Armada approached the southern coast of England, and the use of fireships (floating incendiary vessels), gunfire and, most importantly, a raging storm dispersed the Spanish vessels and drove them up into the North Sea. Parma's invasion force was nowhere to be seen, but as the Spanish vessels floated up by the coast of Scotland, Edinburgh prepared for invasion in its own small way. The town council immediately ordered the raising of a force of 300 men for defence of the city, arming them with musket, sword and pike. The preparations proved unwarranted. Stormy seas pushed the Armada right round Scotland and fewer than 70 ships survived the journey home.

Sovereign Contempt

All of Scotland's monarchs had to tread carefully when dealing with the authorities of Edinburgh, as James VI discovered for himself in 1595/96. In late 1595 James felt himself affronted by the attitudes and sermons of many of Edinburgh's high-ranking clergy and nobles, and consequently ordered the expulsion of 25 of Edinburgh's key citizens from the city, replacing them with a body of eight personal councillors. The decision was announced in St Giles Kirk and was the catalyst for an angry mob, which marched on the Tolbooth where James was sitting with the Lords of Session (he had retreated there on hearing of the gathering crowd). The mood was turning ugly – many in the crowd were armed – and James made his escape. The mob eventually quietened down, and its leaders gained enough composure to write up a petition of grievances for the king's attention. Yet James, who left the city for Linlithgow the next day, labelled the riot treasonous and ordered Edinburgh's Courts of Justice to leave the city in punishment, removing the judicatories to Leith and the Court of Session to Perth.

James returned to Edinburgh on 1 January 1596, treating the remaining magistrates with contempt as rebellious inferiors. His attitude so incensed local authorities that both magistrates and ministers went on strike for

15 days, bringing much of the administrative business of the city to a grinding halt. Eventually James realized that he could be fighting a losing and unpopular battle, and reinstated Edinburgh's Courts of Justice and instead imposed a fine of 20,000 merks on the troublesome city.

The Union of Crowns

On 24 March 1603 Queen Elizabeth I of England died. This event, although it occurred many miles from Scotland, was to have tumultuous effects on the city of Edinburgh and a dramatic change in the government of the entire Scottish nation. With her demise James VI of Scotland inherited the throne of England, so bringing about the Union of Crowns that would eventually lead to England and Scotland being drawn together in the Act of Union of 1707.

For Edinburgh the greatest immediate change was that James quickly left for London, taking with him his royal court and leaving a somewhat subdued city. Hundreds of courtiers, domestic staff, nobles and businesses that had served the monarch in Edinburgh found themselves effectively out of work. Merchant trade dropped, including maritime importations through Leith, as some of Edinburgh's wealthiest citizens moved out into England. Imports from France, Spain and Holland dried up almost entirely owing to subsequent wars between those countries and England, in which Scotland was now involved. (Nor did England compensate Scotland by giving it access to its international trade markets.) James had said that he would return to Scotland every three years, but in the event he only came back to Scotland and Edinburgh once, in 1617 (*see* 'The Return of James

VI', p.94). There was undoubtedly a sparkle gone out of the city with James' absence, and a downgrading of its status within Britain – James liked to say that he could rule Scotland with the stroke of a pen.

The Golden Charter

Charters have always been important in Edinburgh's history. Charters reaching back to the reign of David I helped to shape and define the city in broad ways, from its boundaries and jurisdictions through to its trading rights and customs tariffs and relationship with the monarch. In 1603 another charter was given to the city, this time under the rule of James VI, who had just become James I of England upon the death of Queen Elizabeth. His relationship with the city, from which he had previously ruled Scotland, was now uncertain, and his so-called 'Golden Charter' of 1603 clarified and widened the boundaries of municipal administration. The Charter, a lengthy and complicated legal document, was emphatic in its praise for Edinburgh's citizens: 'we therefore, and in consideration of the good services and affection of the inhabitants of Edinburgh toward us, have resolved to leave in perpetual remembrance thereof, and for the maintenance of religion, virtue and policy within the said town, by not only ratifying and confirming their ancient rights, lands, liberties, and immunities, but to enlarge and endow the same with more privileges and lands, than any other city or town within our kingdom'. The charter extended Edinburgh's legal jurisdiction over Leith and Newhaven, and gave the city more possession over the finances raised within, making Edinburgh one of the most independent civic communities in Britain.

John Napier (1550-1617)

Edinburgh's history is littered with great scholars, and John Napier merits a place in the intellectual pantheon of the city. Born in Merchiston Tower in 1550, Napier was the son of Archibald Napier, the seventh laird of Merchiston, and as a teenager went on to study at St Andrews University. His brilliant academic future was not immediately apparent – he dropped out of university and went travelling in Europe (possibly studying as well) between 1566 and 1571. On his return to Scotland in 1572 he married his second wife. Back in Edinburgh, he then began to produce the intellectual works for which he is remembered. His area of excellence was primarily mathematics, and his work *Mirifici Logarithmorum Canonis Descriptio* essentially invented logarithms, upon which many other sciences have based their mathematical processes. He also pioneered methods of multiplication that became known as 'Napier's bones' (the system used numbered rods) and increased the popular use of the decimal point.

Napier was not just a rationalist, but was also deeply interested in theology, astrology, magic and the occult, frequently attracting the title of sorcerer. One of his eccentricities included using a rooster to deduce which of his household staff might be telling a lie.

Napier died of gout in 1617 and was buried in St Cuthbert's Church in Edinburgh. His name lives on not only in books on mathematics but also in Napier University, Edinburgh, and in several astronomical bodies.

The Return of James VI

Although James VI promised to visit Scotland once every three years after the Union of the Crowns in 1603, his first and only visit to Edinburgh after that date would be in 1617. He arrived on 16 May in grand style, being met at West Port by magistrates and local dignitaries in full ceremonial dress. (The king and his huge entourage had journeyed overland from Berwick to Leith.) The Royal Palace in Edinburgh Castle was completely refurbished both inside and out, and Holyrood Chapel

also received a similar sprucing up. The Town Clerk made an oration to James of quite overwhelming obeisance, referring to the monarch as 'our true phoenix' and 'the bright star of our northern firmament'. Edinburgh's streets were thronged with rejoicing crowds as James made his way through the city, although there were isolated incidents of fighting and anti-royal sentiment (not everyone agreed with the Town Clerk's opinion of James). Thereafter James indulged in much eating and festivities, reminding the city of some of the glamour it had lost when his court had moved to London.

James' visit to Edinburgh was not purely out of love for the city. A parliament was held in the city, which James attended. From his remote position in London, James felt deep suspicion that his desire to plant Episcopalianism firmly in Scotland might be undermined by ministers in the Scottish capital. His visit was partly (or arguably, mainly) an attempt to steer the Scottish kirk back on course – only the next year he attempted to impose his *Five Articles* of Episcopalian practice on Scotland, to much resistance.

Greyfriars Kirk

Nestling to the south of the Grassmarket, Greyfriars Kirk has a central place not only in the spiritual life of Edinburgh, but also in the political history of Scotland. Following the years of the Reformation, Queen Mary granted the land on which the church would be built to the town council, primarily for use as a burial ground. Building work on a new church began on this land in 1602, but it was not until the very end of 1620 (Christmas Day) that Greyfriars Kirk opened to take services. Its name alluded to the pre-Reformation convent that had previously dominated the area. The building itself was simple to behold, being a Gothic-style six-bay structure with stark interior furnishings.

The great historical event of Greyfriars Kirk was its use for signing the National Covenant (*see* p.104) in 1638, and the politics of Anglo-Scottish relations ebbed and flowed around the church for the next half century. In the 1650s, for example, Oliver Cromwell (1599–1658) had his forces use the church as a barracks. Then in 1715 disaster struck. Sensitively, the town council had located a gunpowder store beneath the church, which subsequently blew up and reduced the whole west end of the church to ruin. Rebuilding work went on until the 1720s, and a new church was built on the western side, meaning that Greyfriars now had two separate congregations. Over a century later, in 1845, fire destroyed much of the interior of the church, and subsequent restorations gave the church a more ornate feel, including stained glass. More reconstruction followed in the 1930s, and the dividing wall between the two churches was removed. To this day Greyfriars continues to resound with the sounds of worship, and it remains an important landmark in Edinburgh's past.

Andrew Melville (1545-1622)

L ife did not begin well for Andrew Melville. His father was killed at the Battle of Pinkie in 1547, and his mother died of illness shortly afterwards. Melville's care rested in the hands of his doting brother Richard, who soon began to recognize his younger brother's intellectual gifts. He mastered Greek with extraordinary speed, and went on to study classics and philosophy at the University of St Andrews. From 1564, at the age of only 19, Melville continued his education in Paris then Poitiers, although France's religious turmoil forced him to move to Geneva in 1567, where he was appointed chair of humanities. By this time his learning had expanded impressively, adding oriental languages to his portfolio.

In 1574, Melville decided to return to Scotland once more, and went to Edinburgh. Here Melville was faced with a choice, being offered positions as the principal of St Andrews and Glasgow universities. Melville chose the latter, and famously transformed the university from a failing institution into a place renowned for its learning. Yet he remained intimately connected with Edinburgh, principally as the moderator of the General Assembly, but religion came to be a source of trouble as well as succour in the later years of Melville's life. Problems involving his resistance to Episcopacy led to his fleeing Scotland for a year, after which he became a lecturer then rector of St Andrews. In 1606 Melville was consigned to four years in the Tower of London, having publicly mocked the king and queen in a Latin epigram for what he saw as their superstitious, ostentatious and Romish religious rituals performed in the chapel in Hampton Court. On his release, Melville was prohibited from returning to Scotland, and instead went to Sedan in France where he took a professor's chair and died in 1622 at the age of 77.

George Heriot (1563-1624)

George Heriot was a man of great wealth and of great heart. The first of 10 children, Heriot was born into a family of Edinburgh goldsmiths. Such a business was undoubtedly lucrative, but not always well regarded –

goldsmiths also served as money lenders. Nevertheless, the young Heriot showed commercial talent from the beginning, and soon set up his own business near St Giles Kirk, receiving membership of the Incorporation of Goldsmiths in 1588. The subsequent success and growth of his business brought him into contact with royalty, including King James VI. Hence on 17 July 1597, Heriot became Goldsmith in Ordinary to James' wife, Anne of Denmark, and four years later became Jeweller and Goldsmith to the king, a position that also involved being Royal Pawnbroker and Moneylender.

Such a position brought affluence and influence. He received a new apartment in Holyrood Palace and, when James VI ascended to the English throne in 1603, Heriot moved down to London as Jeweller and Goldsmith at the Court of St James. Heriot was undoubtedly a man of commercial acumen – his nickname was 'jingling geordie', in reference to his extreme wealth. Yet he was also regarded as a kind and considerate man, and one capable of helping those less fortunate than himself. This was demonstrated on his death in 1624. His will, drawn up the year before his death, left the bulk of his estate to the founding of the George Heriot's Hospital in Edinburgh. The bequest, totaling £23,625, was an extraordinary final act of generosity to the city he loved.

Robert Bruce (1554-1631)

St Giles Kirk in Edinburgh has been home to numerous famous clergyman, including Robert Bruce. Bruce was born into a landed family, the Bruces of Kinnaird, but the young Robert had his own path to follow. Despite receiving a good education in the law, and against the wishes of his parents, he took up the study of theology. During this period of Scottish history, being a churchman brought political dangers, and consequently his family asked Bruce to resign his rights to the family estate. This he did without hesitation.

Bruce proved to be a powerful and charismatic preacher, taking over as the minister of St Giles following John Knox's death in 1572, an auspicious and spiritually important post in the city. He also caught the attention of James VI. The king held Bruce as his favourite preacher for a time, and it was such royal approval that probably aided his family's decision to restore him to the full titles of the estate in 1590. Yet Bruce continued to serve Edinburgh, and on two occasions he became Moderator to the General Assembly of the Church of Scotland. Bruce was particularly known for the power of his sermons on the Lord's Supper, which attracted many listeners from across the city and beyond.

Although favoured by royalty, Bruce was no subservient royalist in character. Public criticisms of the king led to Bruce's banishment to France. In 1603 he was granted permission to return to Scotland, although under the condition that he remain within three miles of his family's estate. Edinburgh lost a great preacher. In 1629 he was allowed preaching rights at the small Larbert Church, which soon became packed with listeners. In testimony to his personal power, Bruce's funeral in 1631 attracted up to 5,000 mourners.

REFORMATION &
ENLIGHTENMENT

Charles I (r. 1625-49)

More than possibly any other monarch in British history, Charles I brought out Britain's social and religious divisions, leading it down to the road to civil war and regicide. A full portrait of the life of this failed monarch would be impossible here, but what did he mean for the city of Edinburgh, the capital of the country to which he brought war from 1637?

Charles received his coronation in Edinburgh in 1633, at Holyrood Abbey – after five years of vacillation and argument it was chosen in preference to St Giles Kirk. The night before his crowning he stayed in Edinburgh Castle, and had the honour of being the last serving monarch to sleep in the castle. The event was a typical display of royal pageantry, and the town council had traditionally been loyal to the crown, but relations with Edinburgh would not be so good as Charles' reign wore on. His financial impositions on Scotland, but more so his attempt to impose Episcopalian rituals and a new prayer book through his hated archbishop, William Laud, produced violence and, eventually, outright war. The riot of 23 July 1637 in St Giles was just the beginning of a deep anti-royalism that ran through Edinburgh, and the city became the centre of Covenanter protest (*see* 'The National Covenant', p.104).

Charles made one last visit to Edinburgh in 1641, hoping to quench some of the rebellious fire in the city, but his awkward personality won him few friends. Shortly afterwards Charles' Episcopal structure in Edinburgh was overturned by the Covenanters, and Edinburgh Castle was captured by the Covenanter general Alexander Leslie (1580–1661) in March 1639. The city was steadily opened to Charles' arch rivals (Oliver Cromwell visited and stayed in Edinburgh) while Charles' destiny lay elsewhere – after defeat in the Civil War he was beheaded on 30 January 1649 outside the Banqueting House in Whitehall, London.

Parliament House

Edinburgh's Parliament House was built during the troubled reign of Charles I, who specifically requested a new building that would house the full administrative body of the city of Edinburgh – the Parliament, the Lords of Session and the town council. A location was found between St Giles Kirk and Cowgate (the building actually sat next to St Giles), and Sir James Murray, His Majesty's Master of Works, was the supervisor of the project. Construction of Parliament House began in 1632, but it would take five years to reach completion. The whole edifice was ready in 1639, and little expense had been spared in the building (the final bill was £127,000). The Parliamentary body was to sit in the majestic Parliament Hall, whose oak-beamed roof was designed to evoke the feel of the Parliament Hall at Stirling Castle. Slender turrets at all the principal corners gave the building a robust yet elegant feel.

In 1707, with the Act of Union, the Parliament House lost its function, and it was principally turned over for use as law courts and for library repositories. (It is today home to the Court of Session.) The building also underwent a considerable revamp in the nineteenth century. The architect Robert Reid undertook a major Classical redesign of many of Edinburgh's buildings, and Parliament House received a colonnaded Greek façade during his creation of Parliament Square.

The National Covenant

The Scottish National Covenant was a landmark act of resistance against English rule, and a momentous event in Edinburgh's history. In 1637 King Charles I, along with his unpopular Archbishop of Canterbury, William Laud (1573–1645), embarked on a major programme of religious reform across Britain. For Scotland, this meant the imposition of a new prayer book and several other changes in liturgy that smacked of Catholicism – not popular amongst Scotland's Protestant kirk. The first reading from the new prayer book at the High Kirk of St Giles in Edinburgh on 23 July 1637 produced a riot, and the near stoning of the bishop of Edinburgh, and the wider flames of protest were ignited.

Out of the mass of protesting voices, leading members of the Scottish clergy gradually united themselves, and agreed to draw up a National Covenant, based on James VI's covenant of 1581. This document expressed loyalty to the king, but also stated that religious reform and the imposition of Episcopacy (government by a hierarchy of bishops) was unacceptable.

In February 1638, in Greyfriars Kirk in Edinburgh, leading figures from across Scottish society signed the Covenant, and the document was also copied for wider Scottish readership. In the next three months, most of

Scotland signed up to the Covenant. Charles temporarily backed down, but the die was cast and continuing struggles between Scotland and England led to the so-called Bishops' Wars of 1639–41.

James, Marquis of Hamilton (1606–49)

James Hamilton was born on 19 June 1606 into one of Scotland's most powerful families, with its seat in Hamilton, Lanarkshire. In 1620 he joined his father at the court of James I in London, where he became particularly close with Prince Charles. In 1628 Charles, now king, made Hamilton the Master of the Horse, an important attendant role. Greater military and political service followed, and in 1637 Hamilton became the King's Commissioner in Scotland and was despatched to Edinburgh in an attempt to negotiate settlement with the Covenanters. This was a delicate role – the Edinburgh Covenanters identified Hamilton as an enemy, and even suspected him of a plot to kill their leadership while in the city. Tens of thousands of Covenanters heckled the Marquis during his journey into the city, and he was glad to reach the relative safety of Holyrood Palace. These negotiations came to nothing, and Hamilton led a military force against Scotland in 1639, only to resign as King's Commissioner later that year, and subsequently attempt a reconciliation between the two warring nations.

In 1641 Hamilton visited Edinburgh again with Charles, but while there he was forced to flee by a hardline royalist plot against him. Hamilton was unable to prevent Scotland drifting further away from London, a failure for which the king had him stripped of his titles (he had become Duke of Hamilton in April 1643) and imprisoned. He was subsequently released

in 1646, and later led the Scottish Engager army that invaded England in
July 1648 for the royalist cause. He was defeated by Cromwell at Preston,
and was beheaded at Westminster on 9 March 1649.

The Royal Scots

The Royal Scots was established in 1633 by Sir John Hepburn, who
fulfilled a warrant from Charles I to create a unit for service over
in France. In effect, what emerged was the first infantry regiment of the
line, the Royal Scots acting as a template for the formation of subsequent
regular British Army regiments. The title 'Royal Regiment of Foot' was
given to the regiment in 1684 by Charles II; the 'Royal Scots' title was
only given officially during the nineteenth century.

Service requirements soon took the young regiment away from Scotland.
In 1680 it received a posting to Tangier (where it won its first battle
honour), and the next two centuries saw the regiment widely applied in
other foreign fields, including Ireland, Germany, Canada, the West Indies,
India, Egypt and France. During this service it was heavily bloodied at
battles such as the capture of Montreal (1760), Waterloo (1815) and Alma
in the Crimea (1854). The regiment was no less busy in the twentieth
century, serving with distinction in both world wars and in almost every
subsequent combat zone of the British Army, including Northern Ireland,
the Persian Gulf War (1990–91) and the conflict in Iraq from 2003.

As with all British regiments, the Royal Scots has been through numerous
title changes and reorganizations. In 1949 the regiment was reduced to a

single battalion in strength, and in 2006 it was merged with the King's Own Scottish Borderers to become the Royal Scots Borderers, the 1st Battalion of the Royal Regiment of Scotland. Its connections with Edinburgh, however, remain as strong as ever. Its headquarters are in the city's Dreghorn Barracks, and it maintains a popular museum in Edinburgh Castle.

Auld Reekie

A uld Reekie' – a Scots phrase meaning 'Old Stinky' – may have an air of humorous affection about it today, but in the sixteenth and seventeenth centuries it evoked far more serious emotions in the people of Edinburgh. A period of rapid growth in the Old Town had produced densely packed, decrepit high-rise housing, filled with people living in the most unimaginable disease-ridden conditions. The smoke from coal fires could be seen hanging in a pall over the city at a distance of 80 km (50 miles), resulting in chronic lung conditions. (Some people took advantage of the smoke to conceal illegal activities – by 1777 there were 400 illegal distilleries scattered throughout the city, the smell of alcohol production masked by the smoke fumes.) Sanitation laws were vainly passed, including attempts to stop people literally emptying their chamber pots out of top-floor windows into the street below; considering that some buildings were 12 storeys high, the results weren't pretty. The writer Daniel Defoe noted that people would shout 'Hold your hand!' as they walked down the street to alert those above.

The Old Town was also a physically intimidating environment, a place of hard climate, violence and darkness. Robert Louis Stevenson, writing as late as 1879, noted: 'You go under dark arches and down stairs and alleys. The way is so narrow that you can lay a hand on either wall; so steep that, in greasy winter weather, the pavement is almost as treacherous as ice. Washing dangles above washing from the windows; the houses bulge outwards upon flimsy brackets; you see a bit of sculpture in a dark corner...'. Tough conditions in the Old Town would, in many places, persist well into the twentieth century.

The Great Plague of 1645

Edinburgh's plague of 1645 was not an isolated event – several dozen plagues have swept through the city over the course of the fifteenth to seventeenth centuries (*see* 'The Black Death', p.82). Yet the 1645 epidemic was one of the most devastating, and it killed up to half of the city's population. Old Town was a place perfect for the spread of the disease. Huge numbers of people were packed into unsanitary housing, living alongside the hordes of rats that were the principal transporters of bubonic plague. Once it took hold, the effects were horrific. Bodies littered streets, doorways and rooms, the period from first symptoms to death usually only lasting three or four days. The Edinburgh authorities acted almost brutally in response, but with some measure of sound judgement. The central policy was to separate the healthy from the dying, hence the infamous incident at Mary King's Close, where 300 victims were bricked into their underground close and left to die (reputedly making the close one of Edinburgh's most haunted locations). Huge burial pits were dug across the city in places such as the Burgh Muir and Leith Links, and the clothes and goods of the victims were boiled in huge vats of water

'Bringing round the dead cart'

to disinfect them. In fact, the anti-plague measures were both sound in principal and practice (if desperately hard-hearted by today's standards), and although the effects of the disease were devastating, the epidemic was eventually contained.

Alexander Henderson (c. 1583-1646)

Edinburgh has produced its fair share of religious radicals during its long history, of which Alexander Henderson is one. Born in c. 1583, Henderson trained in theology and took up his first post at the kirk of Leuchars, Fife, in 1612. In 1615 Henderson allied himself with Presbyterianism, which at that time was growing in stridency against Episcopal influences. In 1637 in Edinburgh, Henderson was a major influence behind the riots against Archbishop Laud's attempts to impose a new prayer book of Scotland. He was also a key figure in the drafting of the National Covenant (see p.104) alongside Johnston of Wariston, a lawyer, and in the formation of the Glasgow Assembly.

By the late 1630s Edinburgh was truly the place to be for Protestant activists, and in 1639 Henderson took up a position as a minister at St Giles. (Another St Giles man, Robert Bruce, was probably the key influence behind Henderson's conversion to Presbyterianism.) There he maintained his political influence, being one of the negotiators at the Treaty of Ripon after the Bishops' Wars and at several major negotiations during the 1640s as England and Scotland attempted to reconcile religious differences and political enmities. Henderson was not blindly anti-royal – indeed he developed something approaching a friendship with Charles I, and after the king's surrender to the Scots in 1646 Henderson begged him, unsuccessfully, to accept the Newcastle Propositions for religious and state reform. By this time, Henderson's health was also collapsing – he died on 19 August 1646 and was buried in Greyfriars kirkyard.

William Drummond (1585-1649)

William Drummond was born on 13 December 1585 at Hawthornden, near Edinburgh, and from the start he had good connections. His father was the first laird of Hawthornden (and gentleman usher at the English court), his mother was the sister of William Fowler (1560–1612), a poet and courtier, and his grandfather was formerly Master of Work to the Crown of Scotland. Young William's pedigree presaged a promising future, and he went on to study at the Royal High School of Edinburgh and the University of Edinburgh. (Drummond's bond with the university would remain strong – in 1627 he gave a donation of 500 literary volumes to the university library.) Travel beckoned, as it did to most young men of means, and Drummond spent two years in Paris and Bourges studying law, before returning to Scotland to take over as the laird of Hawthornden in 1610, on the death of his father.

Law and estate management was not to be Drummond's future, however. With the financial security of his position, he indulged his love of poetry, in which he proved to have a talent. He also started mixing with a rich company of fellow poets and literary characters, including Ben Johnson (1572–1637), Michael Drayton (1563–1631) and Sir William Alexander (1567–1640). Drummond was first published in 1613 (*Teares on the Death of Meliades*, an elegy on the death of Henry, the Prince of Wales) and other publications came thick and fast, mostly collections of pastoral-style verse, of slightly imitative style. Later his writing diversified into political pamphlets – he was a devout royalist and wrote in defence of Charles I and royal authority during the English Civil War, including *Irene: or a Remonstrance for Concord, Amity, and Love amongst His Majesty's Subjects* (1638). Drummond was personally traumatized by the killing of Charles I, and he died shortly afterwards on 4 December 1649.

Charles II (r. 1649–85)

Charles II was living in exile in The Netherlands when he heard of the execution of his father, Charles I (*see* p.102) in 1649. Although the Scots had initially fought against the royalists during the English Civil Wars, a growing enmity between the Scots and the Parliamentary English forces had led to Scottish forces offering assistance to Charles I if he accepted the Solemn League and Covenant. Charles I refused, but his son begrudgingly accepted, even rejecting the Episcopal faith, and on 2 August the king landed by boat at Leith, and then proceeded into Edinburgh up the Canongate and High Street to the castle. He was not there long – a Parliamentarian advance under Cromwell, plus his own dissatisfaction with the Covenanters, led to his fleeing north, although the Scottish pursuers soon brought him back under control. He was crowned King of Scots at Scone on 1 January 1651.

After Scottish forces were defeated at the Battle of Worcester (1651), Charles narrowly escaped capture and fled to Normandy. Yet following the death of Cromwell in 1658, and the military intervention of governor of Scotland George Monck (1608–70), Charles was restored as King of England in 1660. The city of Edinburgh greeted the news with festivities, and Charles was proclaimed king at the Mercat Cross on 14 May.

The Restoration (*see* p.115) brought some measure of peace and pageantry back to Edinburgh, although Charles's other restoration, that of the Episcopacy, quickly changed the mood. Charles enacted his revenge within Edinburgh (*see* 'The Killing Times', p.118), but in a less destructive act rebuilt the Palace of Holyroodhouse, where the Duke of York, the future James II, lived from 1680. The kind died five years later in London.

James Graham, Marquis of Montrose (1612–50)

James Graham is one of a long list of nobles to meet a bloody end in Edinburgh. An educated, militaristic man, James Graham took the earldom of Montrose in 1626, but was not destined to hold the title long. During the religious troubles of the 1630s, Montrose signed the National Covenant (*see* p.104) and led Covenanter troops against the English during the Bishops' Wars of 1639–41. Yet despite his service against England, Montrose grew suspicious of some of the motives of fellow Covenanters – he wanted to reject Episcopacy, but feared the men who might become the new masters, particularly the Marquis of Argyll (*see* p.116). In June 1641 he was arrested by the Committee of Estates (a Scottish governing body) for treason, based on his meetings with Charles I in 1639, but he was eventually released in November.

Now Montrose took a major political about-turn. He became a staunch royalist, and actually fought against the Covenanter forces during the 1640s. His running battles in 1644–45 gave Montrose some signal victories, but also a crushing defeat at Philiphaugh in September 1645. This last defeat, and Charles' surrender, drove Montrose into exile in Europe, where he gathered European troops with the intent of taking back Scotland. This he attempted to do in 1650, but was roundly defeated and subsequently captured.

Montrose was executed at Mercat Cross in Edinburgh on 21 May, having been led through the streets on a cart personally driven by the hangman. His head was stuck on a spike at the Tolbooth, while his limbs were sent to other corners of Scotland. Eventually, Lady Jean Napier had his body secretly disinterred, embalmed and sent to his son in a casket, and following the Restoration this body was buried in St Giles Kirk.

The Cromwell Invasion

Having largely defied Oliver Cromwell, the people of Edinburgh had much to fear when his New Model Army marched into Scotland – Scottish forces had battled with Cromwellian troops at bitter engagements such as Dunbar in early September 1650. Cromwell took over Edinburgh and Leith on 7 September, and the city found itself under tight military rule, with several restrictive curfews in place. Scottish forces in Edinburgh Castle continued to resist, however, so the fortification was placed under tight siege, and finally fell in December. Cromwell himself occupied the home of the Earl of Murrie on the Canongate.

One unusual feature of the occupation was that some of the soldiers took the opportunity to preach to Edinburgh congregations; many local preachers were fearful of taking up their former positions in such a spiritually incendiary environment, and Cromwell himself preached a sermon at St Giles. Yet many of the soldiers were rough-hewn men, and those quartered in Holyrood Palace managed to set fire to the building – almost all of it was destroyed during the ensuing conflagration.

The Cromwellian forces also established English parliamentary procedures within the Edinburgh town council, a fact which the local authorities did not seem to resist unduly – at the time of Cromwell's death they were in the process of erecting a large statue in his honour. Yet his death must have come as a relief to many, as the city had been placed under tough taxation to pay for the occupying forces. With Cromwell out of the way, the people of Edinburgh soon had to adjust to the new reality of the Restoration (see p.115).

The Restoration

In Edinburgh, news of the Restoration of Charles II was initially greeted with great celebration. Bells rang throughout the city and the people cheered what they hoped would be a new period of stability after so much desperate bloodshed and unrest. The Edinburgh Parliament once again resumed its functions with all the pageantry of court. One of its first measures was to give the horribly dismembered body of James Graham, the Marquis of Montrose (see p.113), who had been executed for his royalist support in 1650, a decent and solemn civic burial in St Giles kirkyard, although it took several months for all parts of his corpse to be restored to one coffin.

Following Charles's official return as king of England in April/May 1660, the newly restored monarch then proceeded to set right what he felt were some important wrongs north of the border. Although Charles had agreed to the Covenant to gain the kingship of Scotland, he quickly turned his back on such and reasserted the Episcopacy. On 7 May 1662, for example, he reinstated Bishops in the Abbey Church at Holyrood. He also saw that the Covenanters most guilty of complicity with Cromwell were executed, the most notable victim being Archibald Campbell, the Marquis of Argyll (see below). Argyll was just one victim of what became the vicious hunt of the 'Killing Times' (see p.118). One consequence of this persecution was that many of Edinburgh's official church dignitaries suffered revenge violence – the Archbishop was shot at in Blackfriars' Wynd. The Restoration, in short, was a very mixed blessing for the people of Edinburgh.

Archibald Campbell, the Marquis of Argyll (1598-1661)

On 27 May 1661, another noble head was stuck on a spike outside the Tolbooth in Edinburgh. It belonged to Archibald Campbell, the Marquis of Argyll, who had fallen foul of the monarchy he had so long opposed. Campbell became the Earl of Argyll in October 1638 on the death of his father, and became head of one of the most powerful clans in Scotland. Argyll fell out with Charles I over issues of kirk reform, and became a staunch Covenanter, fighting initially against the royalist clans during the fighting of 1638–40, and securing Edinburgh Castle. Argyll's ruthlessness, however, even created enemies within Covenant ranks, particularly James Graham, Earl of Montrose (*see* p.113).

During the troubles of the early 1640s, Argyll extended his power over Scotland and its kirk, but was put on the military back foot once Montrose began his war against the Covenanters – Argyll suffered a major defeat at Inverlochy in February 1645. Only the defeat of Montrose by David Leslie at Philiphaugh on 12 September saved Argyll from being completely crushed. For the rest of the 1640s Argyll trod an opportunistic line as the royalists were steadily defeated during the civil wars and the Covenanters experienced major splits. He allied himself squarely with Cromwell during the latter's occupation of Edinburgh, making more enemies along the way, so when the Restoration finally came in 1660 he was left acutely vulnerable. He was arrested for treason and put in the Tower of London, then sent to Edinburgh for trial, where he was beheaded on 27 May 1661.

James Guthrie (1616-61)

The Reverend James Guthrie was yet another of Edinburgh's citizens that fell foul of the religious struggles of the seventeenth century. Born in 1616 (his birthplace is unknown), he went on to higher education and later became a professor of philosophy at St Andrews University. Religious ministry beckoned, however, and in 1638 he was appointed minister of Lauder. Yet these were troubled times, and in the wake of Charles I's attempt to impose religious reforms on Scotland (*see* 'Charles I', p.102 and 'The National Covenant', p.104), Guthrie signed the Covenant in Greyfriars Kirk in Edinburgh. There he was also appointed to the General Assembly of the kirk, a body of influential Scots opposed to the English reforms.

Guthrie maintained his opposition to religious changes through two turbulent decades, and he met both Charles II and Cromwell to advance the cause of the protesters. For much of this period he lived in Stirling, but in August 1660 events took him back to Edinburgh. On 23 August, he and a group of nine other ministers met there to prepare a petition for Charles II, recommending that he maintain a Reformed church in Scotland. In the changed Restoration climate, that was enough to constitute treason, and he was arrested and held in Edinburgh Castle. At his trial in Edinburgh on 21 February 1661, he was sentenced to be hanged and dismembered, despite his courageous bearing in court. On 1 June 1661, the sentence was delivered – his head was set on the Nether Bow Gate as a warning to others.

The Killing Times

Religious, nationalist and royal passions have made Edinburgh a bloody place throughout its long history, and violence came in full force following the Restoration of the Charles II in 1660. Charles was a king who had some strong motivations for revenge, and in Scotland, and in Edinburgh in particular, he had a readily identifiable target – the Presbyterians and Covenanters, whom he felt had humiliated the crown and forced his hand over Presbyterianism. Charles brought back Episcopalianism to Scotland, imposing bishops, removing the right for kirk congregations to choose their own ministers and undoing three decades worth of Covenanter legislation in the Estates Parliament, which had been re-established in Edinburgh.

Rebellion was the outcome. Illegal meetings of Covenanters were held on the Scottish moors, then, in November 1666, a large group of Covenanters marched on Edinburgh, resulting in a battle with government troops at Rullion Green. The initial rebellion was crushed – 100 Covenanters were killed in the battle, but there began the 'Killing Times' as the government sought to extirpate all rebellious factions in Scotland. The Covenanters suffered further military defeats, particularly at the Battle of Bothwell Brig in June 1679, which cost 400 lives and resulted in 1,200 people being imprisoned in an improvised concentration camp in Greyfriars Kirk, where hundreds died of violence or disease or were executed. The killings continued until the death of Charles II in 1685, by which time up to 18,000 'Covenanters' (the label included wives and children) had been murdered.

A Student Protest

If there was anything likely to stir up strong feelings in seventeenth-century Edinburgh, it was the subject of Catholicism and Popery. For Scotland's large Presbyterian community, Romanist ceremonies and practices were virtually equivalent with devil worship, and there was something of a student tradition for burning an effigy of the Pope on Christmas Day. Students of the Royal College of Edinburgh stated their intention to do so at the Mercat Cross (the traditional site of the burning) on 25 December 1680, distributing leaflets to interested parties. However, at that particular time the Duke of York, the future James II, and his wife were staying at Holyrood Palace. The duke was known for his Catholic tendencies, so magistrates deployed soldiers to the cross to prevent the irreverent ceremony taking place. In this they were partially successful. The city was completely locked down with military personnel, but the undeterred students moved to Blackfriars Wynd, where they delivered a much-abbreviated version of the ceremony, simply igniting the effigy, shouting 'Pereat Papa', then sprinting off into the dark Edinburgh streets.

This was not quite the end of the matter. Seven students were apprehended but eventually released, although there was passionate feeling against the magistrates who prevented the 'proper' ceremony in the first place. On 11 January 1681, the mansion house of Sir James Dick, the city's Lord Provost, located about a mile south of Edinburgh at Preastfield, suffered an arson attack that razed the building to the ground (Sir James and his family were away at the time). All evidence pointed to radical students as the culprits, and despite a stringent search and offers of financial rewards, the offenders were never caught.

James VII of Scotland, II of England
(r. 1685–88)

When James VII/II took the throne of England in 1685, the odds were already stacked against his enjoying a successful reign. Although James had showed himself of brave and honest character during his extensive military service, he was a Catholic in an officially Protestant country, which history indicated was never a good situation. For his entire reign, therefore, he was often set against Parliament, battling to implement Catholic rights and preferences while Parliament fought against them, suspecting the spread of Romanism. The situation became tighter and tighter until the 'Glorious Revolution', when James was forced from office and fled to France, the throne occupied by William III and Mary II.

Although Scotland was relatively peaceful during James' reign (although James had to quash a rebellion by the Earl of Argyll on his ascension), Edinburgh still expressed some of the tensions of that period. James was well acquainted with the city, staying at the Palace of Holyroodhouse in 1679–80 as King's Lord High Commissioner. His most controversial act within the city was the attempted conversion of the Abbey church of Holyrood into a Roman Catholic Chapel Royal. He gave commission in 1687 for the nave of the Abbey to be devoted to the Knights of the Order of the Thistle, a Catholic order, and the design had a Latin cross layout typical of Catholic churches of the period. It was a provocative building, as was discovered during the Revolution that violently arrived in Edinburgh in 1688.

The Revolution

The Revolution of 1688 was, for England, largely a political affair, without serious bloodshed or violence. James's throne was taken over by William III (r. 1689–1702), the grandson of Charles I, and his queen Mary, daughter of James VII/II. In contrast to England, in Scotland passions concerning the Revolution ran much higher, and with the news of William's arrival to take over James's title, tensions spilled over in Edinburgh. (Note that William himself never actually visited Scotland.) The Presbyterians saw the opportunity to undo some of James' Catholic impositions in the city. A huge mob was assembled which marched on the Holyrood Chapel, recently converted by James to a Catholic place of worship. Serious violence ensued as up to 100 armed Catholics attempted to defend the chapel. At least 12 people were killed during the violence, and the chapel was sacked. More violence centred on the castle, in which the Duke of Gordon, allied to James, held out with 120 supporters in a three-month siege from March 1689 – he eventually surrendered on 13 June.

Physical violence was accompanied by deep political change within the city. In March 1689 a 'Convention of Estates' was held in Edinburgh, a body largely dominated by Presbyterians intent on making the most of the political landscape. It issued the 'Claim of Right', an ordinance that declared a future king could be legitimately deposed if he ruled unethically (basically, if he was a Catholic). The body also called for the abolition of the 'Lords of the Articles', a body used by Scottish kings to control the Scottish Parliament. Although William accepted the title King of Scotland in May 1689, he was far from happy with the Convention's restrictions on monarchical power, and the dissolved the Edinburgh Parliament on 2 August.

The Bank of Scotland

Headquartered in Edinburgh, the Bank of Scotland is the oldest surviving banking institution in the United Kingdom, a remarkable achievement when considering the periods of history through which it has lived. The bank was founded by an act of the Scottish Parliament on 17 July 1695, and was aimed to provide banking and credit services to Edinburgh's elite families and merchants. At first the bank enjoyed a complete monopoly over financial services in Scotland, but the use of their money in the Jacobite Rising didn't help public relations, and the monopoly ended in 1716. In 1727 the alternative Royal Bank of Scotland was formed by charter, and so began a period of cut-throat financial competition between the two institutions, each trying to destroy the other. Matters weren't helped by the political turbulence in Scotland at this time – in 1745 the bank was forced to put all its papers into Edinburgh Castle as the rebel forces of Bonnie Prince Charlie occupied the city.

Nevertheless, the Bank of Scotland survived. It should also be noted that the bank had by this time successfully introduced paper money into practical use – it introduced its first notes in 1696 – making it the first bank in Europe to implement this system. During the eighteenth and nineteenth centuries the bank spread branches throughout the United Kingdom, with the first in London opening in 1867. (It established its main headquarters on the Mound, Edinburgh, in 1806.) The bank gained in reputation as it rode out a series of Scottish banking collapses in the second half of the 1800s and continued to thrive throughout the turbulence of the twentieth century, principally through wise industrial investments. In 2001 the bank merged with Halifax Building Society to become HBOS plc.

Thomas Aikenhead (1678-97)

Religion has claimed many lives in Edinburgh over its history, and one of the last to die of official religious intolerance was young Thomas Aikenhead. Aikenhead was born into an Edinburgh medical family, but was orphaned by the age of 10. He went on to pursue a medical education at Edinburgh University, from where he graduated in 1693. Yet it was while at university that he acquired some dangerous ideas. Within the university library were atheistic works by the likes of Spinoza, Thomas Hobbes and Descartes, which Aikenhead read and absorbed. Becoming a committed atheist himself, he acquired several volumes of anti-religious works.

Unwisely, Aikenhead talked with his friends about his views, and one of them reported him to the authorities. His room was searched and he was arrested on the charge of blasphemy in the autumn of 1696. The unfortunate young man was incarcerated in the notorious Tolbooth prison. Only on 23 December was he finally transferred to the Edinburgh High Court under the 1661 and 1665 Scottish Blasphemy Acts.

The trial did not go well for Aikenhead. His friends appeared as prosecution witnesses and his defence was totally inadequate. Terrified by the experience, Aikenhead pleaded mercy on account of his youth, but on 24 December he was sentenced to be hanged. On 8 January 1697 Aikenhead took his final walk to the gallows outside the Tolbooth, some say with a Bible firmly clutched in his hand.

Meal Market Fire of 1700

Edinburgh's layout has always made it vulnerable to fire, and throughout its history several major parts of the city have been reduced to ashes. Although the great fire of 1824 tends to capture much of the press in this area, another major conflagration occurred in 1700 around the area of the Meal Market and Parliament Square.

The Meal Market, located directly to the south of Parliament House, was established by James III in 1477, and grew steadily over the centuries as a vibrant trading zone. It was also a physically cluttered place, with lots of combustible materials lying around waiting for disaster to strike. And strike it did. In 1700 a fire broke out in the lodging of Lord Crossrig at the home of John Buchan, located near the Meal Market. The fire quickly took hold with alarming ferocity, spreading out through the market area and across Parliament Square. As twelve-storey buildings went up in flames, families were seen scurrying for their lives (including a naked Lord Crossrig, clutching his young daughter) – in total 200 families would be made homeless by the disaster. The east and south sides of Parliament Square were burnt to the ground, taking down stately buildings (including the Scottish Treasury Room, the Exchequer and the Exchange) alongside more ramshackle housing. The Bank of Scotland building was also destroyed, but staff and other helpers managed to save virtually all of the important customer documents, allowing the bank to reopen the branch in another part of the city shortly afterwards. After the fire, it took several years to rebuild the area.

Captain Green's Riot

The year was 1702, and as a proposed union between Scotland and England fanned political flames, an incendiary incident occurred that ran from the Firth of Forth and onto the streets of Edinburgh. Feelings were running high amongst Edinburgh's port communities. A Scottish ship of the Darien Company, the *Annandale*, had been seized on the River Thames and sold to the English East India Company without restitution to the Scottish firm. Shortly after this incident, one Captain Green piloted another ship, the *Worcester* – itself belonging to the East India Company – into port at Burntisland on the Forth for repairs. Local people seized the vessel as reprisal for the *Annandale*, but then Captain Green's crew made matters much worse for themselves. Probably as an act of drunken goading, the crew members suggested that they had captured another Darien vessel in Asian waters, and had killed the crew. As it happened, there was a vessel that had been missing for a suspiciously long time.

Captain Green and his entire thirteen-man crew were subsequently arrested and held in Edinburgh, and despite negligible evidence all 14 were sentenced to death. Later, after more sober reflection, the magistrates reprieved the crew, an act that inflamed the Edinburgh mob. On 11 April, a mass of furious locals marched on Parliament Square, and so threatened members of the local council – even the Lord Chancellor was physically attacked – that they were forced to hand over Captain Green and two of his crewman. They were marched down the Canongate to Leith, where they were hanged on an improvised gallows. It is likely that at this time the captain of the supposedly missing vessel was alive and well and living in India.

The *Edinburgh Courant*

Edinburgh being a city of intrigue and upheaval, a reliable source of news was a valued commodity in eighteenth-century Edinburgh. On 14 February 1705 a new source of such information appeared on the streets of the city, the *Edinburgh Courant*. It was a broadsheet newspaper that was the United Kingdom's second regional newspaper, pipped to the post only by the *Norwich Post* of 1701. Its founding publisher was one James Watson and it was later taken over by Andrew Anderson. One of its early editors, however, was none other than Daniel Defoe (1660–1731), the author of *Robinson Crusoe* (1719) and *Moll Flanders* (1722) amongst other works of fiction. The very first edition laid out its credentials for the public with the title: 'The Edinburgh Courant, with the Freshest Advises, Forreign and Domestick. Published by authority.' The imprint continued with the following lines: 'Edinburgh, Printed by John Moucur, for the Undertakers, and to be sold at Mr. John Johnston's house, almost at the foot of Mowbray's Closs [sic], at the Netherbow.'

The paper went through several transformations over subsequent years. In 1710 it was renamed the *Scots Courant*, which remained in print until 1720, at which point it was rebranded again as the thrice-weekly *Edinburgh Evening Courant*. This paper ran until 1873, when the *Courant* title was finally wound up after over 150 years of service to Edinburgh.

The Act of Union

The Act of Union between Scotland and England was the end of a long and tough political process, one made complex by numerous vested interests all trying to pursue their own agendas. To simplify the matter greatly, it was primarily interests of commercial advantage (freedom of trade) and the reassurance of protection for Scottish institutions such as the church and legal system that convinced the representatives of both countries to agree to the Union of 1707. Nevertheless, feelings about the Union ran high, and the days leading up to its confirmation saw riots and violence on the streets of Edinburgh.

For Edinburgh, the Act of Union resulted in the final loss of the city's Parliament, and what seems to be a period of deep dislocation and civic uncertainty. Robert Chambers, a nineteenth-century Scottish writer, called the period immediately following the Union Edinburgh's 'dark age'. He wrote: 'From the union, up to the middle of this century, the existence of the city seems to be in a perfect blank! No improvements of any sort marked the period. On the contrary; an air of gloom and depression pervaded the city, such as distinguished its history at *no* former period.'

Social Plight

By the beginning of the eighteenth century, the living conditions for many of Edinburgh's citizens were utterly intolerable. Much of the city's population was crammed into the terrible dirt and claustrophobia of the Old Town, where they were afflicted by diseases such as typhus and dysentery. One Edinburgh writer of the time observed that every inhabitant had his own dunghill in the streets, opposite his door, and of there being 'many outside stairs projecting from the houses under which swine were kept by the inhabitants, that were allowed at pleasure to wander about the streets, and played a part of scavengers'. The terrible living conditions were compounded by population growth, economic hardship and the legacy of political turmoil. In terms of population, Edinburgh grew from around 25,000 people in 1700 to some 40,000 people in 1745, without a corresponding expansion in housing. Financially, the city was also on the ropes. The Act of Union in 1707 stripped Edinburgh of much of its governmental structure, which had the initial effect of stealing economic strength from a city that was already dependent on its service industries, although these would recover by the nineteenth century. The town council governed available contracts and frequently dispensed them with nepotism and greed. Furthermore, the attempt to establish a Scottish trading colony at Darien on the Isthmus of Panama, collapsed disastrously and thousands of people lost their investments, causing riots on the streets of Edinburgh and other towns.

Such conditions made life in Edinburgh unbearable for many in the early eighteenth century, but eventually forced some degree of change and progress later in the century, including the development of the New Town (see p.132).

The Jacobite Rebellion of 1715

Although James VII/II was never again to return to the throne of either England or Scotland, that did not prevent his supporters rising up against William III and carrying out acts of rebellion during the rule of his successors. Through the reign of Queen Anne (r. 1702–14) and into that of George I (r. 1714–27), resentment bubbled away amongst the Scots, reinforced by heavy taxation imposed from England and the grant of toleration to Episcopalians.

When James VII/II died in 1701, his place for his adherents, the Jacobites, was taken by his son, James Stuart – 'The Old Pretender'. With the coronation of George I in 1714, a Hanoverian who didn't even speak English, a rebellion plan was hatched, and 8,000 Jacobites under the command of the Earl of Mar attempted a military takeover in Scotland, aiming at 'restoring' Stuart. Edinburgh received notice of the attempted coup, and was put on high alert. The town council was generally loyal to the crown – it had fined people for even toasting Stuart's health – and it organized a rudimentary defence. Edinburgh's citizens were armed and trained, the city's fortifications improved, the water levels in Nor'Loch were raised by shutting the sluice, and provisions were stockpiled in case of siege. The preparations were actually enough to deter the Jacobite army from attacking, and they were ultimately defeated in battle by the royalist forces. Edinburgh was proving to be a royally faithful city.

Resistance against the Union would continue in various forms (*see* 'The Jacobite Rebellion of 1715', p.129), but the free trade elements of the agreement did seem to pay off if we take the long-term view. The revenue increase in Scotland between 1707 and the mid-nineteenth century was about 2,500 per cent, three times as much as that experienced in England. Yet many of the civic buildings of Edinburgh are testimony to the days when Scotland ruled itself.

The Young Pretender

The Jacobite Rebellion of 1715 may have been crushed, but Jacobite tendencies still bubbled under Scottish society, and rose forcefully to the surface 30 years later. In 1745 Prince Charles Edward Stuart (1720–

88), the son of James Stuart and known better to history as the 'Young Pretender' or 'Bonnie Prince Charlie', landed with a small military force in the Outer Hebrides, intent on restoring a Stuart to the throne while George II (r. 1727–60) was away in Hanover. What initially began as a foolhardy expedition soon gathered popular support, and with what was eventually a major army, Stuart marched south.

Progress went well (although resistance was not particularly well coordinated), and the city of Edinburgh began putting together a defence in response. Part of the defence was a freshly conscripted 1,000-strong regiment of foot soldiers, with the city's Lord Provost in command. By 15 September Charles's Highland army was on Edinburgh's doorstep, but attempts to bring the Edinburgh garrison out to fight degenerated into farce – most deserted before they even left the city, and those that went outside the city walls swiftly fled. Charles followed up with a bloodless surprise invasion of the city on the early morning of 17 September, where he established himself as King James VIII – although the castle remained in hands loyal to the crowned King George II.

Charles settled into a court at Holyrood Palace, and the city saw a short burst of royal glamour once again. The period was very short, however. After a failed invasion of England, the Jacobites were finally defeated at Culloden in April 1746 by the Duke of Cumberland, and Bonnie Prince Charlie fled to France, leaving Edinburgh firmly without a king.

The New Town

Following the final defeat of the Jacobite rebellion in 1746, Edinburgh's magistrates took a long, hard look at its future. Edinburgh would never again have a royal court, so the authorities considered how to give the city back some of its former prestige and self-confidence. In 1752 Sir Gilbert Elliott of Minto published a pamphlet entitled *Proposals For Carrying On Certain Public Works In The City Of Edinburgh*, which outlined planned building developments for Edinburgh, based closely on the renovation ideas of George Drummond (1687–1766), who frequently held the Lord Provost position in the city between 1725 and 1764. The plans were excitedly accepted, and so began one of the seminal building projects in Edinburgh's history. New structures included the Royal Exchange (*see* p.143) and St Cecilia's Hall, but even these were overshadowed by the greatest development of them all – New Town.

New Town utilized Barefoot's Park to the north of the city, now accessible since the draining of the Nor'Loch and with the subsequent building of the North Bridge. Designed by James Craig and implemented along with other figures such as Robert Reid and William Sibbald, the New Town was a modern development of Classical style and space, designed around ordered parallel streets. The streets of the New Town have become some of the most commercially desirable in Edinburgh, including Princes Street and George Street. With the creation of the New Town, Edinburgh regained some of its former sparkle, and, set against the Old Town, truly created a city of two halves.

Building Bridges

With the steady creation of the New Town, Edinburgh required bridges to create more efficient links through and across the developing city. One of the most important of these was North Bridge, which would run across the newly drained Nor'Loch and thereby form a direct connection between the Old Town and the New Town. Its foundation stone was laid in October 1763 and construction began in 1765. It was, and remains, a magnificent bridge with its three arches crossing a distance of 346 m (1134 ft) at a height of 21 m (70 ft). The bridge first opened in early 1769, but a partial collapse in August of that year, which killed five people, lead to further extensive renovations and it was finally completed in 1772.

North Bridge was not the only impressive span to emerge in eighteenth-century Edinburgh. Inhabitants of Edinburgh's southern parts benefited from the construction of South Bridge, running down through the Old Town from High Street. Despite being a nineteen-arch structure, the bridge was built in only two years (1786–88), impressive when compared with the ordeal of North Bridge. A later link between the Old Town and the New Town, set to the west of North Bridge, came in 1836 with the George IV Bridge leading off from the Lawnmarket, and also the Waverley Bridge connecting Market Street with Princes Street. These bridges were integral to Edinburgh's expansion, and changed the ebb and flow of the city.

Encyclopaedia Britannica

The *Encyclopaedia Britannica* is today an international phenomenon. The oldest English-language encyclopaedia still in print, it was actually born in Edinburgh in 1768, a product of the intellectual passions of the Enlightenment. It was the idea of two men, Colin Macfarquhar, a local Edinburgh printer, bookseller and businessman, and Andrew Bell, an engraver who would provide illustrations. They were assisted by William Smellie, a 28-year-old scholar, writer and editor who put together many of the first articles.

Together their idea was for an encyclopaedia that would rival anything produced on the continent. Between 1768 and 1771 the first edition of the encyclopaedia was produced in 100 parts (each part equating to pamphlet size), eventually bound together in three volumes of 2,391 pages in total. The encyclopaedia's format – long, authoritative articles set in alphabetical order – was a hit with the public, aided partly by controversy over some of the work's more graphic medical engravings.

From its promising Edinburgh beginnings, and fuelled by a savvy system of updates and persuasive sales staff, the *Encyclopedia Britannica* grew into an international sensation, crossing the Atlantic and passing through numerous stages of ownership, including the Edinburgh publishers A&C Black. The twentieth century saw intense financial challenges for the publication, particularly from print and eventually internet competition, but it has managed to survive (primarily through making itself available in DVD format) and is still one of the greatest single print repositories of knowledge.

Register House

Register House, as its name implies, was built to house Edinburgh's Public Records (the town's public archives). Prior to the construction of Register House, the records had been kept in poor conditions within the Inner Session House, where they suffered from the depredations of rodents and damp. The idea of a purpose-built repository had been floating around since the early 1700s, but it wasn't until 1765, following determined representations from the Edinburgh authorities, that the Treasury finally granted £12,000 for the building.

Built at the end of the North Bridge, the Register House can be viewed in light of the general expansion of Edinburgh during the Enlightenment (*see* 'The Age of Enlightenment', p.137), augmenting the construction of the New Town. The architects on the project were the great Robert Adam and his brother James, and the foundation stone was laid on 27 June 1774. (Although the Adams Brothers visited the site every year, the construction was supervised by James Salisbury, the clerk of works.) In 1778, however, the project ran out of money, and for six years it remained unoccupied in a nearly completed state. Only the government provision of an additional £15,000 enabled the building to be finished for occupation, and it began its official use in 1788.

Since its completion, and like many other buildings in Edinburgh, it has undergone a series of 'improvements', including a rear extension in 1820s and modifications to the front to allow for more efficient passenger traffic. Nevertheless, it remains a classic Georgian building.

A Class Divide

Prior to the development of the New Town (*see* p.132), Edinburgh was a truly mixed palette of classes. Within the Old Town, the commoners and the people of rank almost literally rubbed shoulders. The houses of nobles in places such as Milne's Court were but a stone's throw from far less salubrious streets. Common street traders were able to earn a living from passing gentry, while dubious taverns were accessible to those of the upper classes who wanted to slip away for rough entertainment.

With the arrival of the New Town in the second half of the eighteenth century, the social as well as the physical fabric of the city was changed. Now there was a definable locale for people of status, a place of more space, light and cleaner air. Inexorably, the monied people of the Old Town began to shift to the north. A.J. Youngerson, in his encyclopaedic work *The Making Of Classical Edinburgh* (1966), describes the subtlety of the transition: 'All this gradually changed. The better-off withdrew to George Square, or to the New Town. For a time, all their servants had still come to the markets in order to purchase their everyday requirements; and the lawyers, of course, had still come to Parliament Close, or conduct at least some of their business, in the traditional manner, in convenient taverns in or near the High Street.' Yet as Youngerson further points out, the New Town quickly acquired its own shops and businesses, and soon the wealthy could live in near isolation from the Old Town. The change resulted in a less colourful, more decorous city, and the Old Town sank into poverty, deterioration and spiralling crime.

The Age of Enlightenment

The Age of Enlightenment was a Europe-wide phenomenon, a time of accelerated learning and a departure from some of the previous theological confines of knowledge into new areas of science, literature, economics and philosophy. For Edinburgh, the Enlightenment was arguably the point of its transition into modernity, as the city became one of the most intellectually fascinating cities in the United Kingdom. Late eighteenth-century and early nineteenth-century Edinburgh produced some of the greatest minds the United Kingdom had (or has) ever seen, including scientists such as William Cullen (1710–90), James Hutton (1726–97) and Joseph Black (1728–99), writers such as Oliver Goldsmith, Robert Burns (1759–96) and Sir Walter Scott, the great political economist Adam Smith, and artists of great renown, including Allan Ramsay Jr (1713–84) and Sir Henry Raeburn (1756–1823).

For Edinburgh, one of the key conditions of the Enlightenment was a new political stability that enabled free thought to flourish. Once the Jacobite rebellions had been quenched, the city generally settled down in terms of its relationship to the English monarch, and most of the Enlightenment thinkers had pro-royal credentials. In fact, Edinburgh's Enlightenment figures, particularly its painters, often relied heavily on royal patronage for their livelihood, and many of them moved down to London to take advantage of the court. Nevertheless, Edinburgh was astonishingly vital throughout this period, and some of the work that emanated from the city would change the intellectual map of the world.

Enlightenment Societies

As Enlightenment intellectualism spread throughout Edinburgh, it was natural that the city's academic elite would filter itself out into societies promoting particular agendas or lines of enquiry. Numerous learned societies evolved or were founded, some of which survive to this day and still have an influence on the intellectual landscape.

One of the early groups was The Select Society, formed in 1754 by 15 prominent Edinburgh intellectuals, and originally called the St Giles Society.

The objective of the society was, according to its founding principles, 'the pursuit of philosophical enquiry and the improvement of the members in the art of speaking', and its membership was glittering, founding members including Allan Ramsay Jr, David Hume, John and James Adam (1732–94), George Drummond and Adam Ferguson (1723–1816). The group did not last long – its last meeting was in 1763 – but by then there were other societies also thriving. Many of the members of The Select Society moved into The Poker Club, the group ostensibly focused on promoting the formation of a local militia, but also given over to general intellectual debate.

A lasting Enlightenment society is the Royal Society of Edinburgh (RSE), an organization that still exists today to promote and fund original Scottish research. It began life as the Philosophical Society of Edinburgh in 1737, devoted to a broad range of intellectual activities, from medical matters to theology. In 1783 a royal charter transformed the group into the RSE. The list of societies mentioned here is far from exhaustive – others included the Rankenian Club (which also influenced the formation of the RSE) and the Wernian Society, which was more focused on science and natural history – but they all helped to put Edinburgh on the intellectual map of Europe.

The Royal Infirmary of Edinburgh

The Royal Infirmary of Edinburgh (RIE) has an ancestry stretching back into the eighteenth century. Its origins can be traced to 1725, when the Royal College of Physicians of Edinburgh acted to establish a hospital for the city's poor. The idea had been propagated since 1712, but now the Royal

College utilized reassigned shares from the closure of a local fishing company, plus donations from wealthy benefactors, to found a small 'Hospital for the Sick Poor' on Robertson's Close, off Cowgate, in August 1729.

The ailing masses of Edinburgh benefited from this small institution for six years, at which point came greater recognition in the form of a royal charter in 1736. The charter attracted wealthy benefactors, and encouraged the growth of the institution. Between 1738 and 1741 a new 228-bed infirmary was built in Jamaica Street (now Infirmary Street), and a new surgical hospital was constructed in the 1830s. The second half of the nineteenth century saw the RIE take up another new site, on Lauriston Place, the location taking advantage of the cleaner air towards the edge of the city. Construction of the new building took place between 1870 and 1879, with the previous infirmary buildings being demolished in 1884.

Since the late 1800s, the RIE progressively expanded at Lauriston Place, becoming one of the United Kingdom's premier hospitals. Nevertheless, in the late 1990s plans were passed to build a brand-new infirmary at Little France, south-east of the city, while the Lauriston Place site was sold to property developers in 2001. The new building, which officially opened in 2003, serves not just Edinburgh, but the whole Midlothian and East Lothian region.

The Coat of Arms

A coat of arms is a badge of both identity and authority. Although Edinburgh's great and good had used several armorial emblems throughout history, the city was destined to receive its official coat of arms in 1732. It was granted by the Lord Lyon King of Arms, the Scottish official responsible for regulating and issuing heraldic symbols and issuing grants of arms. In its original form it stayed until May 1975, when it was modified by the City of Edinburgh District Council, and further tweaks in design came later in 1996, when the City of Edinburgh Council was formed.

The central element of the coat of arms is a shield depicting, according to official nomenclature, 'Argent, a castle triple-towered and embattled Sable, masoned of the First and topped with three fans Gules, windows and portcullis shut of the Last, situated on a rock Proper'. The castle and rock are natural symbols of Edinburgh, both being at the centre of the city's origins, and the shield is flanked by two figures – a maiden and a doe or hind, rearing up against the shield on the right. The maiden alludes to Edinburgh Castle's medieval appellation of *Castrum Puellarum* ('Castle of the Maidens'), probably a reference to the castle's function as a residence for princesses, and its use in parts as a nunnery. The doe or hind is the symbol of St Giles, patron saint of Edinburgh. The Latin motto on the crest – *Nisi dominus frustra* – translates as 'Unless the Lord, then in vain', being a contraction of a verse from the 127th Psalm.

The Porteous Riots

The Porteous Riots were a classic example of why it is wise not to take on the eighteenth-century Edinburgh mob. In early 1736, two local men – Andrew Wilson and George Robertson – were arrested and sentenced to death for smuggling and the theft of goods from the custom house at Pittenween. At the time, Scotland was chained by tough British excise duties and taxes, giving the condemned men considerable popularity amongst the people. This popularity rose when both men made an escape attempt from Edinburgh's Tolbooth Church in March; those about to die were encouraged to think of the afterlife, and they had been taken there for a service. Robertson escaped but Wilson, possibly preventing guards chasing after his friend, remained destined for the gallows.

On the day of his execution – 14 April – a large and volatile mob gathered, angrily voicing their support for Wilson as he was led to the Grassmarket for his execution. A detachment of the City Guard, led by

the arrogant and some say wine-fuelled Captain Porteous, was there to provide security. Wilson was executed, but what happened next is less clear. It appears that some boys threw stones at the hangman (this was something of a tradition), and the crowd grew hostile. In disproportionate response, Porteous ordered his reluctant men to open fire on the crowd, killing up to nine people. For this act Porteous himself was arrested and condemned to death, but his execution was granted a stay by royal intervention. Deciding to take matters into its own hands, an incensed mob stormed the Tolbooth prison on 7 September, seized Porteous and hanged him in the street.

Edinburgh Exchange

In the mid 1700s, Edinburgh's officials began studying ways in which to make the streets of the city less crowded with traders and market stalls. They arrived at the idea of a purpose-built merchants' exchange in which all the trading could be confined behind an attractive façade. A location had to be found, and the search was helped by the ruinous condition of a block of tenements off the north side of High Street. It was resolved to demolish these to make way for the new Exchange. To sweeten the plan for financiers, the proposal included plans to build official administrative buildings, such as a library for the Faculty of Advocates and some premises for the Lords of Session.

Finally the proposal achieved the necessary permission and finance to go ahead, and building work began in August 1753. The Exchange building itself was designed by John Adam (1721–92) and another local Edinburgh architect, John Fergus. It was a striking Classical-style building, with a huge sculpted pediment braced below by four Corinthian pilasters. Inside was an expansive court for holding the merchants and a large Custom House for use by magistrates. Work was finally completed in 1761 at a cost of £31,500. Ironically, the creation of this large building never really solved the problem of street traders, and the Exchange was eventually bought in its entirety by the town council and came to be part of what is known as the City Chambers, largely devoted to civic matters.

The Cross of Edinburgh (Mercat Cross)

M ercat crosses are found throughout Scottish cities, towns and villages. They essentially mark the place where markets would gather for trading (in many places they still do), but in Edinburgh the Mercat Cross gracing the Royal Mile found many more uses, including some particularly unpleasant ones.

The current Mercat Cross in Edinburgh dates back to only 1885, and was built there under the instruction of Prime Minister William Gladstone (1809–98). From the octagonal crosshouse stands a shaft based upon the fifteenth-century original – indeed the shaft actually incorporates parts of the original, which stood just a short distance from the present-day monument (its position is marked on the floor). Over the centuries Edinburgh's Mercat Cross was not only a focal point for traders, but also for public announcements (some announcements are still made today at the Cross) and, grimly, as a place for many of Edinburgh's public executions. The people killed there included murderers such as John Dickson, who killed his father in 1558 and following his execution had almost every bone in his body smashed by an iron bar at the Cross. They also included some of Edinburgh's most famous victims, such as James Graham, the Marquis of Montrose (1650) (*see* p.113) and Archibald Campbell, the Marquis of Argyll (1661) (*see* p.116). Little wonder that many say the old Cross site is a haunted location.

Nor'Loch

The Nor'Loch was a man-made creation. In 1460 James III, concerned that Edinburgh was most vulnerable to attack from a northerly direction, ordered that the ground between Princes Street and the Old Town was flooded to create what was in effect a huge moat on the north side of Edinburgh Castle. The flooding was achieved by damming off the eastern end of the valley and then diverting water into it from St Margaret's well. All went according to plan, and in fact the Nor'Loch was initially a pleasant addition to the City, a place of rest and recreation. (It was, however, also used for the 'sousing' of suspected witches, although for some that would doubtless be an afternoon's entertainment.)

Yet with the march of time the loch became, by contrast, an eyesore and a hindrance. It was used as a dumping ground for the city's waste, including human excrement and animal parts from slaughterhouses. Build-ups of methane gas would leak into the nearby houses, causing illness and delirium. Furthermore, it critically restricted northward development of the city, which by the eighteenth century was becoming ever more claustrophobic.

In 1759 the decision was taken to drain the loch and so create a better passage between the Old Town and the developing New Town. The drainage began in 1765 and took many years before solid ground emerged to create what is today the Princes Street Gardens. During the drainage process a footway was created across the boggy ground, and this was supplemented on a huge scale by rubble from the New Town construction, leading to the creation of the artificial hill called the Mound, now home to the Scottish Royal Academy and The National Art Gallery. The draining of the Nor'Loch, plus the building of the new North Bridge (*see* 'Building Bridges', p.133), undoubtedly gave Edinburgh room to breathe.

Allan Ramsay (1686-1758)

Scotland has long been known for its literary output, and Edinburgh was home to one of the great Scottish poets in the Enlightenment – Allan Ramsay. Ramsay was born in Leadmills, Lanarkshire, in 1686 but moved to Edinburgh in 1700 following the death of his mother. His initial vocation as a young adult was wigmaking, and he opened his own wig' shop in the Grassmarket. Yet around this time Ramsay also began writing poetry. He founded a poetry society called Edinburgh's Easy Club, a society peopled with fellow poets, almost all with Jacobite political leanings. The club's members all took pseudonyms, and Ramsay's was 'Isaac Bickerstaffe' and later 'Gavin Douglas'.

By 1716 Ramsay was beginning his publishing career, printing poems in local broadsheets, and in 1718 he also converted his wigmaking shop into a bookshop. In the mid-1720s, however, he moved his premises to

Luckenbooths, and established what was the first circulating library in Edinburgh. Alongside his successful career as a bookseller, his efforts as a poet and playwright flourished. His most influential poems, songs and plays include the *Tea Time Miscellany* (1724), *The Ever Green* (1724) and *The Gentle Shepherd* (1725) – the latter was a pastoral play that four years later was performed to music. Ramsay actually opened his own theatre, but Presbyterian opposition to any sort of fun eventually resulted in the theatre closing. Ramsay died in 1758, having spent the last years of his life living around Castlehill. He was buried in Greyfriars kirkyard.

Oliver Goldsmith (c. 1730-74)

Oliver Goldsmith was not a citizen of Edinburgh, nor was he was a Scot. He was, however, one of the intellectual characters of the Enlightenment who added some additional colour to eighteenth-century Edinburgh. Born in Ireland about 1730, Goldsmith was destined to become a venerated poet, playwright and novelist, although his early life gave no suggestion of the greatness to come. He bounced through several academic institutions during his teenage years, known for being reckless with money and socially awkward, although he still managed to graduate from Trinity College Dublin in 1749. A career now beckoned, but Goldsmith would have several false starts, including an attempt to emigrate to America (he missed the ship) and a stab at practising law in Dublin (he gambled away all his money before he could start the course).

It was then that Edinburgh drew in the dissolute young man. At the age of 24 he went to study medicine at the University of Edinburgh.

Although Goldsmith did attend some lectures, the vivid nightlife of the city provided an irresistible distraction. Goldsmith joined a student group called the Medical Society and made associations with fellow Irishmen, both proving good drinking companions in Edinburgh's many bars and taverns. Goldsmith spent two winters in Edinburgh before heading to the continent to complete his medical studies. After wandering for many years, he found himself in London in the 1750s and his prodigious literary output began, going on to write great works such as *She Stoops to Conquer* and *The Vicar of Wakefield* (amongst a huge variety of hack work). It was a fine conclusion to an otherwise ribald life, a life that ended in London in 1774.

David Hume (1711-76)

David Hume stands as one of the great names of Enlightenment philosophy. He was born in 1711 in Edinburgh to a deeply religious family, Calvinistic values being imbued in the boy by his mother. She was also his tutor until he turned 11, when he attended the University of Edinburgh. He spent the next four years at the university, and on graduation a career in the law seemed to be his future. But Hume was deeply fascinated by philosophy, and was also experiencing critical doubts in his religious faith. Hume engaged himself in private study, avidly reading treatises sceptical towards Christianity. Between 1734 and 1740 Hume wrote his *Treatise of Human Nature* (part of this time Hume lived in Anjou, France). When published, the work was unspectacular in terms of sales, but did invite controversy with its rationalist and anti-theistic views.

Hume published further works in the early 1740s, and in 1744–45 seemed likely to take up the position of Chair of Moral Philosophy at the University of Edinburgh. However, deep opposition from Edinburgh town council and local ministers resulted in Hume's candidacy for the position being rejected, much to his chagrin. After a short period as secretary to General St Clair and embassy postings in Vienna and Turin, Hume became librarian of the Advocate's Library in Edinburgh in 1752, and also managed to maintain a strong output of philosophical writing. His great works include *Enquiry Concerning Human Understanding* (1748),

Enquiry Concerning the Principles of Morals (1751) and *The Natural History of Religion* (1779; published after his death), all accompanied by decent amounts of controversy. Hume again travelled in Europe, but eventually returned to his much-loved Edinburgh, dying there in 1776 at the age of 65.

Allan Ramsay Jr (1713-84)

Allan Ramsay Jr came into the world with a promising genetic make-up – his father was poet Allan Ramsay Sr (*see* p.146). Yet while his father had a literary bent, Ramsay Jr leaned towards artistic expression.

The young Ramsay, who was born in October 1713 in Edinburgh, showed considerable talent in languages when he attended the Edinburgh High School. Artistic talent also emerged, and Ramsay went on to study at Edinburgh's Academy of Saint Luke from 1729 and then under the tutelage of Hans Hysing (1678–1752), the Swedish portrait painter who was living in London. Portraiture was to be Ramsay's primary skill as an artist, and in 1732 he established his own studio in Castlehill, Edinburgh, from where he executed portraits for wealthy local personalities.

From the mid-1730s, Ramsay began to indulge a fondness for travel to the great artistic centres of Europe. In 1736–37 he moved through Italy, living in both Rome and Naples where he continued his studies under Italian masters. Ramsay then moved to London, a place where he built his reputation as a portrait artist and attracted the business of many wealthy patrons, including Archibald Campbell, the 3rd Duke of Argyll (1682–

1761). With a new-found wealth Ramsay moved back to Edinburgh in 1753–54, then spent another three years in Italy before heading back to London. His career now reached exceptional heights, painting portraits of the Prince of Wales and receiving the appointment as Principal Painter to the King in 1767. In 1773, however, an accident injured his right arm and he could no longer paint. He died on 10 August 1784.

Adam Smith (1723-90)

Adam Smith is a philosopher and economist whose theories still carry enormous influence today. Although primarily known as an economist, his intellectual interests were exceptionally wide. He wrote and lectured upon ethics, jurisprudence, language and rhetoric, with his great works including *The Theory of Moral Sentiments* (1759) and *Lectures on Jurisprudence* (1776). Yet one work in particular stands out above all the rest – *An Inquiry into the Nature and Causes of the Wealth of Nations*, which Smith published in London in 1776. This work provided not only the theoretical framework of modern economics, and defined concepts such as the free market and the division of labour, but also had a direct impact on the way Western governments have controlled fiscal policy.

Smith has deep associations with the city of Edinburgh, although he also spent long and important periods of his life in Oxford, Glasgow and also in France. Smith was actually born in Kirkaldy just to the north of Edinburgh, and after studying in Oxford he began lecturing in Edinburgh from 1746, where he befriended David Hume (*see* p.148) and also attended the Enlightenment society known as The Poker Club of Edinburgh. In 1751

Smith began a long period at the University of Glasgow, but returned to Edinburgh in 1778, after which he became a founder of the Royal Society of Edinburgh. Smith died in the city on 17 July 1790, and was buried in Greyfriars kirkyard.

Robert Adam (1728-92)

Robert Adam left his mark on Edinburgh in the most literal of ways. In Edinburgh alone this great Neoclassical architect and interior designer is responsible for the design of some of the city's august landmarks, including Register House (see p.135), Charlotte Square, No.8 Queen Street and the Old College of the University of Edinburgh (see p.86).

Adam's life was intimately bound up with Edinburgh from his earliest years. He was born in 1728 in Kirkaldy but his family moved within a year into Edinburgh itself. Adam's father was William Adam, a stonemason and architect, and both his brothers (James and John) also grew up to be architects and designers. Robert was educated at Edinburgh High School and then attended the University of Edinburgh from 1743. After his graduation in 1746, he worked with his father as an apprentice, then with his brother John as a partner in the family business after William died in 1748.

In 1750 the Adam brothers won a major contract to decorate the grand state apartments at Hopetoun House west of Edinburgh, and other important Scottish projects quickly followed. Adam then went on to further his architectural knowledge in France and Italy, returning to Britain in 1758 and establishing another architectural business, this time in London. Such was his skill that in 1761 he was appointed Architect Of The King's Works. The last years of Adam's life were prolific, but tragically he died of a burst blood vessel in his stomach on 3 March 1792.

James Boswell (1740-95)

Edinburgh, and Scotland in general, has few figures more culturally famous than James Boswell. Born in the city in 1740, Boswell was the son of Alexander Boswell, Lord Auchinleck (1706–82), and was equally well-born on his mother's side. His childhood was characterized by a coldness from his parents, with an austere Calvinist ethos pervading the Boswell household. Boswell nevertheless flourished academically, and in 1753 (aged only 13) he entered the University of Edinburgh where he studied law and art, and upon his graduation he divided his time between Edinburgh and London. His father forced him to take a position in the University of Glasgow in 1759, but Boswell defied the order and headed down to London.

By this time Boswell was already producing essays and writing an erudite journal, building the foundations of what would be an impressive literary legacy, and in London he met and befriended Samuel Johnson, the man who would inspire Boswell's most famous work. Yet Boswell was as interested in enjoying life as writing about it. He travelled widely in Europe, picking up stories, drinking heavily, womanizing (and acquiring venereal diseases) and meeting intellectuals such as Rousseau and Voltaire. Eventually he returned to Edinburgh in 1766, where he began to practise law.

Through all his ribald adventures, Boswell produced a stream of literary works. These included essays for the *London Magazine*, travel/picturesque literature such as the *Journal Of A Tour To The Hebrides*

(1785) and his most famous work, *The Life of Samuel Johnson*, published in 1791 after the death of Johnson in 1784. Boswell's literature is known for being as earthy as the man himself, and as such did not always please the literary establishment. In his final years Boswell fought against depression, alcoholism, gambling and illness, and he died in London in 1795.

Robert Burns (1759-96)

R obert Burns is as much a national icon of Scotland as he is a poet and lyricist. He was born into a poor family on 25 January 1759 near Ayr, although his cash-strapped father ensured that the young Burns received a good education. Nonetheless, as Burns grew older his life was one of physical rather than intellectual labour, working on a series of failing family farms between the 1760s and 1780s. Burns's romantic career was more successful, and his production of illegitimate children and affairs with various local girls earned him much social disapproval. Yet by this time he was also writing fine poetry, and in 1786 he published a volume entitled *Poems, chiefly in the Scottish dialect*. Burns actually intended to use the proceeds to help him emigrate with his pregnant lover, Jean Armour. Yet its success persuaded him to stay, and he moved to Edinburgh, where he was appreciated as a new literary sensation. He quickly published a second volume of poems, and also wrote well-received collections of romantic letters. After 18 months in Edinburgh, he went off on travels around Scotland and also began work amassing a huge collection of traditional Scottish songs, an activity that contributed to Burns's high national status today.

Despite Burns's creative bent, farming was still a persuasive draw on him, and in 1788 he once again attempted living from the land. This failed, and he found employment thereafter in the Excise in Dumfries. Yet by this time his health was failing and he, although not his legend, died on 21 July 1796.

Adam Ferguson (1723-1816)

Adam Ferguson was one of the figures who made Edinburgh such an intellectual centre of the British Enlightenment. He was actually born in Logierait, Perthshire, and was educated in St Andrews and Edinburgh universities, emerging eventually with a degree in divinity. His initial vocation was as a chaplain in the Black Watch Regiment, but his faith steadily weakened and he eventually returned to academia. In 1757 he returned to Edinburgh, first as librarian to the Faculty of Advocates then moving on to take two professorships in the University of Edinburgh, first in natural philosophy (from 1759) and later in moral philosophy (from 1764).

While the subjects he taught are not as familiar to us today, essentially Ferguson was involved in what we would call sociology. Ferguson not only analyzed the themes that united human behaviour, but also those that created diversity and social stress. He also looked at the social effects of economic realities, such as how the division of labour was a primary force in the financial and intellectual progress of human society, although at the same time he recognized that such a division was also a force for inequality and strain, and also for emotional vices such as envy and jealousy. Ferguson's output included *An Essay On The History Of Civil Society* (1792) and *Essays on the Intellectual Powers: Moral sentiment, happiness and national felicity* (1805).

Ferguson did not spend his whole intellectual life within Edinburgh's confines – he travelled around Europe with the Earl of Chesterfield and also visited America. He suffered a stroke in 1780, however, resigning his chair five years later, although he did not die until 1816.

Sir Henry Raeburn (1756–1823)

Sir Henry Raeburn was one of the true masters of portrait painting during the Enlightenment, and one of Edinburgh's most renowned artists. He was born in Stockbridge, Edinburgh, on 4 March 1756. Although he was born into a relatively comfortable home, this did not protect him from some of the hardships endured by many families of the eighteenth century. When only a few years old he was orphaned, and was subsequently brought up by his older brother William. He received an education at Edinburgh's Heriot's Hospital, and in his mid-teens he began work as a goldsmith. At the same time, the naturally artistic boy began to paint miniature pictures. His talent attracted the attention of several leading artists, including David Martin (1737–97), at that time Edinburgh's top portrait artist, and later Sir Joshua Reynolds (1723–92). In the meantime, Raeburn married Anne Leslie, a wealthy widow, in 1778, and he was able to indulge his artistic talents more fully. He travelled to Italy in 1784–87, and when he returned he established a successful painting business. His subjects included Walter Scott, Adam Smith and

David Hume. Such was his recognition that in 1815 he was elected to the Royal Academy and in 1822 he was knighted by George IV (r. 1820–30). Raeburn died in July 1823, but his collections still attract thousands of art lovers to places such as the Scottish National Portrait Gallery.

Sir Walter Scott (1771-1832)

Walter Scott is at the heart of the history of the British novel and is arguably Edinburgh's most famous literary figure. He was born in Edinburgh on 15 August 1771, and apart from frequent visits to his grandfather's farm in the Borders, his childhood was spent in the city. He was educated at Edinburgh High School and Edinburgh University – at the latter he took a law degree and was called to the Bar in 1792. Yet while he established a career in the law (he later became Sheriff-Depute of Selkirk and a Principal Clerk to the Court of Session), it was his literary output that gave him true social definition. He began writing and translating during his mid-20s, focusing on collections of stories and ballads and poetry. He published a collection of Scottish ballads in 1802, after which he published on a regular basis and became a leading figure in Edinburgh culture, being one of the founders of the *Quarterly Review* in 1809. It was for his historical novels that he became most well-known, particularly from the publication of *Waverley* in 1814. His other novels included *Ivanhoe* (1819), *The Talisman* (1825) and *The Heart of Midlothian* (1819), while other Waverley titles included *Rob Roy* (1817) and *Quentin Durward* (1823). Such was his enormous success that he was even chosen as organizer for King George IV's visit to Edinburgh in 1822 (*see* 'A Royal Visit', p.167).

Scott subsequently went through a period of financial hardship in the 1820s, and he died at Abbotsford, Melrose (where he lived) on 21 September 1832. Edinburgh would never forget him (*see* 'The Scott Monument', p.181).

Alexander Nasmyth (1758-1840)

A lexander Nasmyth holds the highest of ranks amongst Scottish landscape painters. Born in the Grassmarket in September 1758, Nasmyth was educated in Edinburgh and quickly developed an exceptional artistic talent that took him to the Trustees' Academy. His first artistic employment was with a coachbuilder, decorating the sides of the vehicles with heraldic art, but his ability brought him to the attention of the great Allan Ramsay Jr (*see* p.150). Ramsay took the young Nasmyth down to London to foster his talent, and in 1778 Nasmyth was competent enough to return to Edinburgh to set up his own practice as a portrait artist. One of his patrons, Patrick Miller of Dalswinton, lent Nasmyth sufficient money to complete his education by spending two years (1782–84) in Italy.

His return to Edinburgh, however, was not triumphant. Henry Raeburn had taken over as the city's supreme portrait artist, and Nasmyth's liberal political views were alienating him from his more conservative client base. In order to make financial ends meet he took up various projects, including some architectural work (he designed the Dean Bridge and St Bernard's Well), and switched much of his artistic focus to landscape work. In this genre Nasmyth flourished, painting with boldness and scale and investing the images with faithfulness to nature. His work brought him official recognition. He was a member of the Royal Society of British Artists and of the British Institute between 1801 and 1839, and was granted membership of the Royal Scottish Academy in 1834. Nasmyth died in 1840, but has subsequently been titled the 'father of Scottish landscape painting'.

Sir David Wilkie (1785-1841)

The Trustees' Academy in Edinburgh provided the schooling of many of Scotland's great artists, including Sir David Wilkie. Wilkie was actually born in Cults, Fife, on 18 November 1785 and almost immediately showed an intense love of art. This was to the displeasure of his father, who wanted his son to follow a more practical vocation. Nevertheless, Wilkie Sr was eventually persuaded to send David to the Trustees' Academy, where he refined his artistic talents between 1799 and 1804.

Following his education in Edinburgh, Wilkie then attended the Royal Academy in London from 1805. He developed a fascinating ability with character studies, all informed with a homely Dutch style that gave an impression of intimacy and realism. His paintings included *The Blind Fiddler* (1807), *The Village Festival* (1812) and *The Scotch, or Penny Wedding* (1818), and together with Henry Raeburn (*see* p.157) he helped bring Scottish artists more to the recognition of wider society in the United Kingdom (he was also he was appointed His Majesty's Limner for Scotland in 1823). He became financially successful through the sale of prints of his artworks.

At the peak of his success in the mid-1820s, Wilkie experienced some misfortunes, including deteriorating health and financial loss through the bankruptcy of his printmaker. To recuperate, he spent the next three years travelling through Europe and the Middle East, where he also acquired a bolder, more Romantic style of painting that still appeals to this day. Wilkie died suddenly on a return journey from Alexandria in 1841, although his art lives on to this day in Edinburgh's galleries.

The Friends of the People

The French Revolution inspired many British radicals with the possibilities of common enfranchisement. In April 1792, the English Society Of The Friends Of The People was formed, principally composed of Whig politicians seeking constitutional and parliamentary reform. While this group was principally led by politicians, an alternative version sprang up in Edinburgh in July 1792 with a far more democratic structure. This was known as The Friends Of The People Society, and on account of reduced subscription rates it was manned mainly by professional artisans and workers, ranging from tailors to tanners. The society grew to wield respectable power. It held 'general conventions' for its membership and that of the English society, and it so intimidated the town council that it was frequently dispersed by troops. For example, the third general convention, held in October 1793 in Edinburgh's Grassmarket, called for universal male suffrage, but was stopped by the authorities and several of its leaders were deported to convict settlements in Australia. Members also rioted over local issues, and generally the violence limited the amount of popular support the society could gain – middle classes in particular found the disruptive personalities unacceptable. Society members also hatched seditious plots. In 1794, for example, two extremists, Robert Watt and David Downie, hatched a plan to take over the city of Edinburgh, even ordering 400 pikes as weapons. They were finally apprehended – Downie was transported abroad, but Watt was executed. Such crackdowns on political radicalism steadily reduced the power of the society, until it faded from view.

Leith Docks

Leith's access to the oceans has always been critical to Edinburgh. Without the port at Leith, Edinburgh would have never enjoyed the international trade on which it grew. Yet by the early eighteenth century the dock facilities needed significant upgrading if they were to cope with increased traffic levels. A new stone pier was built in 1701, and other dock facilities were added in the 1720s and 1770s. Building of Leith's first wet dock, however, did not commence until 1801, having been delayed on several occasions for financial reasons. Following a government loan of £25,000 the foundation stone was finally laid on 14 May 1801.

Little did people suspect at the time, but the new development would become a crippling financial burden rather than a blessing. Between 1799 and 1813 the town council borrowed a hefty £240,000 to develop the docks, in addition to the government investment (although the government was in fact just another creditor).

The new dock facilities opened between 1806 and 1817, but there were many criticisms about their quality from the sailors who used them, and who often used alternative dockyards along the Scottish coastline. The debt spiralled out of control, and in 1833 the city of Edinburgh effectively went bankrupt (although the docks were only one source of debt for the city). Government intervention steadily restored the situation, and Leith docks soldiered on. During the twentieth century it faced some tough times, industrial unrest and a decline in trade leading to the dock area becoming a rough and dangerous haunt. Nevertheless, recent regeneration programmes have seen the dock area smartened into a lively and accessible part of the city once more, with plans (at the time of writing) to build 16,000 homes in the area, alongside major shopping and commercial developments.

During the Napoleonic Wars

The Napoleonic Wars, as well as requiring Scotland's military manpower for campaigns, also had an unexpected result for the city of Edinburgh. British victories in various campaigns, particularly after the battle of Waterloo in 1815, resulted in the netting of tens of thousands of French prisoners, many of whom were transported over to captivity in England and then in Scotland. In the search for a secure Scottish site of incarceration, one dour and forbidding location offered itself naturally – the dungeons of Edinburgh Castle.

Conditions for the French prisoners at Edinburgh seem to vary considerably, and often depended upon the status of the person involved. For those consigned to the darkest recesses of the dungeons, ill health and high mortality were certain cellmates. (Recent renovation work near the dungeons has frequently been interrupted by workers reporting, amongst other spectres, the ghost of a French drummer boy.) In some cases 40 prisoners would be confined in a single vault, their only sleeping quarters being hammocks slung between rafters. Indeed the problem of overcrowding quickly became critical as the dungeons reached capacity. The overflow was displaced outwards to villages, where the French prisoners often had to adjust to the hard life of the Scottish rural poor. Yet many also interacted fully with the locals, teaching them French cooking techniques, taking on jobs to earn money and even putting on French plays for the locals. Even the individuals within the dungeons were enterprising, producing artifacts from whatever materials were available, including wood, stone and straw. Items produced include 68-gun model warships, musical instruments, human figures and even wooden stamps used to forge currency. These people were some of the last to be imprisoned in Edinburgh's castle.

'Scotland's Shame'

The National Monument was intended to be a place of quiet reflection, built to remember all those who had lost their lives fighting in the Napoleonic Wars. Its location, chosen in 1822, was to be Calton Hill, and the plans for the monument were very ambitious indeed. It was intended to create a version of the Athenian Parthenon, a beatific Classical vision that was very much in keeping with the Victorian architectural mindset.

The architect chosen for the job was William Playfair (1790–1857), who even though only in his 20s was a rising star within Scottish architecture.

Building began in 1826, at a time when many other building projects were underway in Edinburgh, all vying for public and private money. A total of £42,000 was needed to undertake the project, but building work began before that had been collected. Eight massive stone columns were erected, so big that each stone section for each column needed 12 horses and 70 men to transport it from Craigleith Quarry. It was an enormous, expensive project, and money was running out. Eventually the project ground to a halt, with only £18,000 in the development purse.

The National Monument, dubbed by some 'Scotland's Shame' on account of the frugality that prevented its completion, remains incomplete to this day. Yet it still manages to capture some of the peace and serenity intended by Playfair, hence it remains a popular haunt for daytrippers and those wanting to unwind.

Search for the Royal Regalia

It is hard to imagine how one might lose a near priceless set of royal regalia, but that is nevertheless what happened in 1707. The Scottish 'Honours' consist of a crown, ceremonial sword and sceptre, all bedecked with jewels and crafted in precious metals. The three items date from the late fifteenth and early sixteenth centuries, and the Sword of State and Sceptre were presentation gifts to British monarchs from different Popes.

For many the Honours represented Scottish identity and independence, which in Scotland's shifting political history made them controversial objects. Cromwell unsuccessfully hunted for them during his invasion of Scotland, during which time they were used to crown Charles II at Scone before being spirited away to Dunnottar Castle. With the Restoration, however, Charles was able to return them to Edinburgh Castle, but the Act of Union in 1707 robbed the jewels of their lustre, and they were locked in a chest in the Crown Room and subsequently lost for over a century.

In 1818, the hunt for the Honours was spurred by the Prince Regent (the future George IV). He commissioned none other than Sir Walter Scott with the task – the prince had been very impressed with Scott's work and Romantic nature – and Scott rose to the challenge. He eventually found them in a neglected strongroom in the castle, still in their wooden box. The magnificent jewels were subsequently put on display, and are today on show in the castle.

Union Canal

During the age of the Industrial Revolution, canals were the ideal method for the transportation of goods across Britain. Edinburgh needed to find a way of transporting coal and lime into the city from Scotland's coalfields, and a canal provided the ideal solution. Construction on what would become known as the Edinburgh and Glasgow Union Canal began in 1818, with its building work estimated at a total cost of £240,000. Four years later, when the canal opened for service, the actual cost was £461,760. Nevertheless, the canal was a masterpiece, stretching 51 km (31.5 miles) from Edinburgh to the Forth and Clyde Canal at Falkirk, not only providing a coal route but also creating a through route between Edinburgh and Glasgow.

The canal was an engineering triumph, as despite its chosen route undulating by 73m (240 ft) there were no locks used, except at the connection with the Forth and Clyde Canal, where 11 locks stepped down 34 m (110 ft). Such a 'flat' canal was possible through effort and expense, including cutting a 631 m (2070 ft) tunnel and the construction of three very large aqueducts. Yet sadly the advent of rail transport was soon stripping the canal of custom, and the vehicle traffic of the twentieth century was the final nail in its commercial coffin. The canal officially closed in 1965, but in the 1990s it was reopened under a major project known as the Millennium Link. Scotland had rediscovered the value of its canal network.

A Royal Visit

By 1822 it was high time that Edinburgh received a visit from the monarch. No reigning king or queen had graced the streets of the city since the eighteenth century, so King George IV's visit, planned for August 1822, sent a ripple of excitement through Edinburgh society. What was most notable about the royal visit was the man appointed as chief organizer – the Edinburgh writer Sir Walter Scott. George was a reverential fan of Scott's writing, and also of Scott's intimate and passionate understanding of Scottish people and tradition. At a time when George's popularity in England was flagging, Scott was given the task of preparing a visit that would bolster George's image north of the border.

Scott prepared an elaborate sequence of pageants and celebrations, all of them celebrating traditional Scottish identity. He persuaded the king to wear full belted plaid, and created a pageant in which all the nobles of Scotland wore the same, thus reinvigorating the wearing of tartan, which had largely been confined to Army use since the Jacobite rebellions. Scott also diarized a series of increasingly splendid events, which began on 12 August, the king's birthday, with a procession of the Royal Regalia from the castle to Holyrood Palace. The king himself arrived by ship at Leith on 15 August, and travelled in a large military procession into the heart of Edinburgh, amidst cheering crowds. The subsequent festivities ran for a fortnight from 15 August, and included spectacular events in almost every major civic building in Edinburgh. The highlight for many was George's appearance in Highland dress, wearing pink tights to mask his chubby legs. It was grist for the caricaturist's mill, but there is no doubting that when festivities ended Scott had every reason to be pleased with the magisterial event.

Cholera Outbreak

Cholera, a disease that thrives in unsanitary conditions, was always going to give congested nineteenth-century Edinburgh a hard time. It arrived in England in 1831, cutting a swathe through the population of cities such as Liverpool, and in 1832 it had worked his way northwards and started to do its damage in Edinburgh. The effect was worse, naturally, in the slum areas, and in total some 1,065 people within the city died of the illness, and thousands were hospitalized. Panic spread amongst the population, and in some cases there was even localized rioting in protest at what was seen as a lack of government response to the epidemic.

The Edinburgh Board of Health did issue advice to the public over preventative measures against disease. Some of this was sound, including instructions about keeping body and home as clean as possible, although the mechanism of cholera's actual transmission was still not understood. Other advice was less helpful: a printed notice issued in November 1831 included the caution that 'Experience has shown that the most essential precaution for escaping the disease is sobriety – that intoxication during the prevalence of the epidemic is almost sure to be followed by an attack'. To be fair, as cholera is primarily transmitted through infected fluids, no doubt present in Edinburgh's taverns, the advice was not entirely misplaced, but it is interesting that several councils in Scotland and England took the cholera epidemic as an opportunity to wag the finger against alcohol.

The epidemic died out later in the year, but returned on several more occasions. The Edinburgh health authorities gradually made the connection between sanitation and cholera, and combined with the provision of immediate free health care during the epidemics, cholera was relegated to a regular, but not catastrophic, visitor.

VICTORIAN
& MODERN

The Victorian Era

For Edinburgh, the Victorian era was a period of mixed fortunes. On the one hand, the city undoubtedly shared in something of the prosperity of the empire, and it became known for its professional services (such as banking, legal, financial and publishing) and lively middle class culture (*see* 'The Industrial Revolution', p.175). Yet conversely, for many citizens on the lower rungs of the social ladder, the squalor of life intensified as more people were packed into the Old Town, which at the same time received less and less investment.

Queen Victoria ascended the throne in 1837, by which time the population growth Edinburgh experienced in the first quarter of the century had flattened out. This resulted in a reduction of building within the Old Town, meaning that more people were crammed into the same available space. Studies found that in some places up to 11 people were living in single rooms. Yet in the more affluent New Town, new building proceeded apace. Furthermore, Edinburgh was expanding outwards to create fresh suburbs. This process began with Stockbridge in the 1850s, but soon Edinburgh was forging new developments at Newington, Marchmont and Morningside. The effect of the new suburbs was to heighten the contrasts of Edinburgh, separating the better off from the squalor of life in the older parts of town. Only in the twentieth century was this contrast ironed out to a greater degree.

Building the Railways

The nineteenth century saw the railway network spread across the United Kingdom like a spider's web. For Edinburgh, the first thread to run through its territory was the Edinburgh–Dalkeith line, which ran from the Midlothian coalfield past the south-east of the city and on to Leith. This line was completed between 1831 and 1838, and the traction was provided either by horses or by fixed engines. Despite its sedate reputation, by the 1840s it was transporting 300,000 people every year, but still Edinburgh itself was virtually untouched by the railway.

All this changed with the advent of steam railways, and the city authorities looked for ways in which central Edinburgh could be networked. The big changes came in the 1840s. In 1842 a main Edinburgh–Glasgow line was opened, working from a new terminus building built – against much local opposition – at the east end of Princes Street. Other lines came thick and fast. The Edinburgh, Leith & Newhaven also opened in 1842, connecting Canonmills (New Town) to Newhaven harbour. In 1848 the rail network linked Edinburgh to more distant traffic: the North British Railway began running from Edinburgh to Berwick upon Tweed in 1846, and the Caledonian Railway provided travel between Edinburgh and London (via Carlisle and Carstairs) from 1848. Numerous suburban lines and links were subsequently opened during the 1860s and 70s.

Unlike many cities, the coming of the railways to Edinburgh did not fuel an industrial revolution, although it certainly facilitated the easier transport of coal to Leith docks. What the railways did achieve, however, was to make a growing city more accessible within itself, and to Scotland and England.

Rise of Tourism

Today the city of Edinburgh pulls in some 13 million tourists every year. They come from all over the world, attracted by proud landmarks such as Edinburgh Castle and the city's art galleries. The origins of Edinburgh's tourist explosion, however, date back to the Victorian period. Prior to the eighteenth century, Scotland had appeared as a remote, wild and politically dangerous place for English tourists. Yet several events during the nineteenth century served to change this perception. Firstly, the royal visit by George IV in 1822, plus Queen Victoria's regular trips to the city (and her long stays at Balmoral), gave Edinburgh status and attraction amongst English middle-class travellers. Secondly, and possibly most importantly, the wealth of Romantic literature produced by Scottish and Edinburgh-based writers painted Scotland in a new light. Literary Scotland was picturesque and beautiful, but also gothic, sinister and moody, and this compelling combination soon attracted literate travellers to Edinburgh. (The intellectual output of the Enlightenment also placed Edinburgh on the map.) Wealthy English tourists, moved by the tales of writers such as Sir Walter Scott, were soon flocking into the city.

The development of the railway links between Edinburgh and London from the 1840s provided an alternative means of travel to road and boat – by the 1890s there were three independent lines running up into Edinburgh from southern England. Railways also made travel to Edinburgh more accessible to the masses, with the result that Edinburgh was receiving some 100,000 visitors a year by the end of the nineteenth century.

Industrial Revolution

The Victorian era was a time of stellar growth in industrial output in the United Kingdom, one of the key factors that enabled a small island nation to became the centre of a vast empire. Individual cities and regions throughout the United Kingdom often had their own distinctive industrial mark, such as pottery production in the Midlands, steel manufacture in Sheffield, cotton making in Manchester and shipbuilding in Glasgow. Even during this period of great industrial expansion, however, Edinburgh was dominated by its middle classes in white-collar professions. In 1830 the male middle-class population of Edinburgh was over 20 per cent of the total population – the average for most other cities in Britain was about one in eight. Much employment for these people came from Edinburgh's vast civic administration, but they also delivered the professional services in publishing, law and finance for which Edinburgh became rightly renowned. One effect of this prevalent middle class was that a large proportion of the population had stable salaries, and this in turn fed a healthy trade in luxury consumer goods in the city.

Yet it is wrong to say that the Industrial Revolution passed Edinburgh by entirely, and equally wrong to say that the engine of the city was entirely white collar. Engineering, textile and clothing production and food and drink manufacture still provided for a huge proportion of the workforce.

In 1871, for example, while nearly 33 per cent of Edinburgh's workforce were employed in professional, domestic or commercial work, 64 per cent were working in an industrial capacity. The key difference from other cities, however, is that Edinburgh was not dominated by a single industrial sector, a fact that allowed its professional sector to thrive.

Population Explosion

Prosperity tends to bring population growth in cities, not only from foreign migrants looking for work, but also from increased birth rates and rural people deciding to leave the dirt of the land for the sparkle of the town. During the nineteenth century Edinburgh also saw this trend, although some curious patterns emerged over the length of the century.

In 1801 the population of Edinburgh, according to census figures, stood at 67,288. Yet within only 30 years that figure made a huge leap to 136,054. The primary cause behind the jump was immigration from Ireland. The potato famine there had displaced huge numbers of people abroad, looking to escape, and Edinburgh was a good choice of destination – its diverse employment structure meant that there was work to attract many different types of skills. The effect of Irish immigration was pronounced, for by the mid-part of the century about one per cent of the population of Edinburgh had been born in Ireland. An ingress of rural Scottish and northern English workers into the city also fed the expansion.

Yet the picture of population growth between 1831 and 1861 is far different. By 1861 the population had grown by only another 30,000, a dramatic slowing compared to earlier times. This slowdown is only partly explained by a reduction in immigration. The fact also remained that the big industrial cities such as Glasgow offered mass employment for labourers – by 1871 Glasgow had more than double Edinburgh's population. Population figures did rise considerably at the end of the century, but it seems that Edinburgh largely escaped the huge sustained growth of many other cities in the United Kingdom.

The Great Fire of 1824

The Great Fire of 1824 did levels of damage to Edinburgh's streets and buildings scarcely seen at any point in its previous history. Although Edinburgh had development much since the days of 'Auld Reekie', large areas of the city still consisted of densely packed housing, much of it still with the timber structures so loved by urban outbreaks of fire.

The fire itself began on 15 November 1824 in a seven-storey building at the head of Old Assembly Close, the building serving as a printing house. Spurred on by printing chemicals, the fire soon gutted the building and radiated outwards to other structures. The blaze destroyed the offices of the *Courant* newspaper and was heading towards the Old Town, devastating all the buildings on the south side of High Street when, by noon on 16 November, it seemed to come under control. It was not to be, however. As the first died down, another ignited in the Tron Kirk a short distance from the first fire. The leaded steeple gave excellent fuel to the fire, and the entire church was quickly ravaged. Nor was this the end of the destruction. A third fire broke out on the evening of 16 November in an eleven-storey building on the south side of Parliament Square. This building and many others around it, including the Jury Court Room, were gutted over several hours before the fire was finally brought under control, although there were several small outbreaks for some time afterwards. The total cost of the fire was high: 10 people killed, dozens injured, over 500 families homeless, and £200,000 worth of damage.

The Royal Scottish Academy

The Royal Scottish Academy (RSA) building was originally the brainchild of a group known as the Scottish Academy, founded in 1826 by a group of 11 Edinburgh artists. (The RSA title came with a royal charter in 1838.) The original intentions were to provide a focal point for the promotion and exhibition of fine art, with plans to hold an annual exhibition, deliver education to aspiring artists and host a fine art library. Building of the RSA venue, a Neoclassical-style colonnaded temple known as the Royal Institution, began in 1823 with the laying of the foundation stone on the junction of the Mound and Princes Street. Designed by the great William Playfair, the building opened for use in 1826, hosting its first annual exhibition the following year. Playfair, however, was involved in a subsequent round of enlargements that increased the size of the building in the 1840s.

Organizations who used the early RSA building included the Institution for the Encouragement of Fine Arts, the Scottish School of Design, the Society of Antiquaries of Scotland and the Royal Society of Edinburgh.

The RSA itself moved into the new and adjacent National Gallery buildings in the 1850s, but in 1910 the demands of space meant that the RSA moved out into the Royal Institution building, and the building itself was renamed the Royal Scottish Academy. Together with the National Gallery, the RSA is a major attraction for art lovers in the heart of Edinburgh, and to this day it continues to hold vital exhibitions.

The Burke and Hare Murders

Edinburgh has had more than its fair share of grisly historical episodes, but the Burke and Hare murders of 1827–28 have always had a peculiar hold over the popular imagination. In the early days of anatomical research, there were few means by which scientists could get hold of cadavers for research. Only with the passing of the Anatomy Act of 1832 was a legal system of corpse acquisition put in place – before that time physicians had to rely on other means altogether.

Which leads us to the grim case of William Burke and his accomplice, William Hare. These two opportunistic thieves were employed by Dr Robert Knox, lecturer in anatomy at Edinburgh University, to go grave robbing for corpses, the first transaction taking place in December 1827. Yet the enterprising Irishmen were not taking bodies – they simply murdered victims to order, targeting those whom they felt would not be missed. In total, they murdered 15 people until locals became suspicious, resulting in investigation and arrest. The trial began in December 1828. Burke was found guilty of murder and was hanged,

The execution of William Burke

while Hare was released, having gained immunity by promising to testify against Burke. Knox, though charged with no crime, gained special vilification and was socially ostracized. In a final gruesome twist, Burke himself was dissected by anatomists after his execution on 29 January 1829.

The Scott Monument

In 1832 the great Scottish writer Sir Walter Scott died at the age of 62. As one of Edinburgh's towering literary citizens, Scott had achieved a fame that many felt deserved a lasting monument. So it was during the mid-1830s that a competition was set by the city to design a fitting memorial. Of the many talented civic designers that entered the competition it was George Meikle Kemp (1795–1844), a joiner and draughtsman by trade, who eventually won. In 1840 the foundation stone of the monument was laid, and it would take four years for the magnificent structure to be completed.

The gothic vault, located on the south side of Princes Street, rose 61 m (200 ft) up into the Edinburgh air and access to the top – where spectacular views were to be found – was provided by a flight of 287 steps. It also included 64 statuettes depicting characters from Scott's novels. In a moment of high tragedy, however, Kemp fell into the Union Canal during a foggy day and drowned before seeing his monument completed. The final stone was laid by Kemp's son, Thomas.

Occupying the monument is a statue of Scott himself, in erudite pose. Cut in Carrara marble and having dimensions more than twice life size, the statue was selected by John Steell (1804–91), later Sir John and HM Sculptor for Scotland. The Scott Monument is another great Edinburgh landmark, and a restoration programme in the late 1990s brought it back to its full glory.

The Disruption of 1843

On 18 May 1843, a large group of 450 religious ministers could be seen marching purposefully down George Street, Edinburgh, having left the Church of Scotland General Assembly at the Church of St Andrew. Their destination was Tanfield Hall at Canonmills, and once there they held a meeting that ultimately led to the establishment of the Free Church of Scotland.

The events that led to this meeting showed how volatile Scottish religious feeling could be. The Church of Scotland, born out of the Scottish Reformation in 1560, developed various schisms during its lifetime. One of those schisms revolved around the issue of 'patronage'. Although the Church was technically free of state control, the right of patronage allowed wealthy lairds to impose their own minister upon a congregation, regardless of his qualities.

This situation was tolerated until 1834, when the more radical evangelical wing of the Church gained a majority control over the General Assembly. They rejected patronage, and the refusal of the parish of Auchterarder to accept the patron's nominated minister, Robert Young, blew up into a fiery test case over the issue. Young took his cause to the Court of Session and won the ruling. The Court also enforced its state right to select candidates

– for the evangelicals this went directly against the founding principals of the Church of Scotland. So it was, after several more years of angry debate, the Disruption of 1843 began, and on 23 May the dissenters held the *Signing of the Act of Separation*, creating another branch of Scottish spirituality that still exists today.

The Electric Telegraph

The electric telegraph, developed in earnest during the 1830s, was a revolutionary technology for the United Kingdom, and subsequently the world. Never had communication been so rapid between distant locations, and for Edinburgh – set such a long way from London – the telegraph promised to integrate it further into the economic life of the nation.

Although messages could be transmitted electrically (at first by Morse Code) from 1836, a critical leap in the development of the electric telegraph came from Alexander Bain (1811–77). Bain, a passionate inventor, had been educated in Edinburgh, and in 1841 he created what we would today class as a form of fax machine – an electric telegraph system that was capable of transmitting both words and pictures. In 1846 he improved on the invention with the chemical telegraph, which when refined could transmit just over 1,000 words in less than a minute.

Bain ran one of his telegraph lines between Edinburgh and Glasgow in 1841 and by the end of the decade the Scottish capital was part of a

Alexander Bain

telegraph network over 3,200 km (2,000 miles) long and linking 60 cities throughout the United Kingdom.

Of course, it should be noted that even as Bain was working on his inventions, one Alexander Graham Bell (1847–1922) was born in Edinburgh on 3 March 1847. This graduate of both Edinburgh's Royal High School and the University of Edinburgh would go on to obtain the first US patent for the telephone, the most revolutionary invention in the history of human communications.

National Gallery of Scotland

Set on the Mound between Princes Street Gardens, the National Gallery of Scotland is a striking work of art in its own right. Columned like a Roman temple in the Neoclassical style so loved by Victorian architects, the Gallery had its cornerstone laid on 30 August 1850 by Prince Albert (1819–61), but the building (designed by William Playfair) was not declared complete and open until 24 March 1859.

The Gallery opened hosting a large collection of fine art and books, much of the collection representing the finest of Scotland's artistic talent stretching back over hundreds of years. It proved a big hit with the public, and expansion was soon necessary. The National Portrait Gallery was founded in 1882, although not opened until 1889. In 1906, an act of government also allowed the National Gallery to use the entirety of the building for its collection. Previously it had shared the building with the Royal Scottish Academy (RSA), but the act moved the RSA out into the adjacent Royal Institution building, which then took the RSA name.

Expansion would seem inexhaustible over the next 100 years, and some of the collection was displaced into external buildings, such as the National Gallery of Modern Art (now in Belford Road) and the Dean Gallery opposite that building, which houses sculpture and Dada and Surrealist art. Development is still underway today – not surprising when individual exhibitions alone have attracted over 130,000 visitors. It remains one of Scotland's most popular tourist attractions.

Greyfriars Bobby

The facts about Greyfriars Bobby are uncertain, but there is no doubting that this small Skye Terrier has become one of Edinburgh's most enduring popular heroes. The story begins with John Grey, a night watchman for the Edinburgh City Police who lived and worked in the city from c. 1850. John was married with a young son, also called John, but John's constant companion was Bobby the terrier, who for two years accompanied his master on his rounds, never leaving his side whatever the weather or circumstance.

After some seven years on the beat, John contracted tuberculosis, and died from it on 15 February 1858, leaving a young family and a masterless dog. Grey was buried in Greyfriars kirkyard, and now Bobby began the routine for which he became famous. Rain or shine, winter or summer, Bobby refused to leave the grave except for one excursion away for a meal, which was taken, so people said, at the sound of the One o'Clock Gun (see opposite). The kirk gardener actually erected a shelter across John's grave to provide the dog with some measure of protection from the elements.

Bobby's devotion drew large crowds, and would ultimately prove to be his salvation. A dog licensing bye-law passed in 1867 stipulated that all unlicensed dogs had to be destroyed. Facing imminent destruction, Edinburgh's Lord Provost, Sir William Chambers, stepped in and paid the licence himself – effectively Bobby was now owned by the city. Bobby kept his vigil until his death in 1872, aged 16. A year later a statue of Bobby was unveiled outside Greyfriars, the legend reading 'Greyfriars Bobby – died 14th January 1872 – aged 16 years. Let his loyalty and devotion be a lesson to us all'.

The One o'Clock Gun

Every weekday at one o'clock precisely, an artillery gun fires from the battlements of Edinburgh Castle, giving the city a useful (albeit forceful) mechanism by which to mark the day. The origins of this custom reach back to the early 1860s, when a Royal Navy captain named Captain Wauchope designed a system to allow ships in Leith harbour – 3.2 km (2 miles) distant – set their clocks accurately (the ability to do this was important for navigation). On Nelson Tower, atop Calton Hill in Edinburgh, he constructed a large metal ball that ran up and down a vertical pole. The ball was synchronized with a clock in the Astronomical Observatory near the tower to drop at one o'clock, and provide a long-range visible marker to sailors as to the correct time.

The only problem was that on days of poor visibility the ball simply couldn't be seen. So it was that Charles Piazzi Smyth (1819–1900), Astronomer Royal for Scotland, attached the ball mechanism to the firing mechanism of a cannon on the castle ramparts via a 1,219-m (4,000-ft) cable, providing an auditory means of identifying the hour.

The first firing of the time gun, in June 1861, was a disaster, with three misfires, but eventually the gun became the regular heartbeat of the city of Edinburgh, and remains so to this day. The gun itself has changed several times over the years, from a muzzleloading cannon, to a WWII-era 25-pounder to the modern 105mm Light Gun, and the elaborate cable firing system has been replaced by accurate timing. Nevertheless, the function of the gun has remained the same, and it looks set to be a long-standing Edinburgh tradition.

Heave Awa' Hoose

While the mid-Victorian period was a fine time for the construction of public buildings, the same could not be said of much urban housing. The Industrial Revolution had crammed hundreds of thousands of Scotland's citizens into dilapidated urban sprawl, and Edinburgh was no exception. The Old Town in particular was a housing nightmare. Many of the buildings there dated back 300 years, and were in a woeful state, with crumbling foundations and deep cracks running through weight-bearing walls. The problem was compounded by the fact that most of the area's wealthy citizens were long gone, moving out into the New Town and its most salubrious and status-sensitive environs. Building collapses became commonplace, but without people of influence in the area the Old Town was starved of development funds.

On 22 November 1861, an event brought the terrible state of Edinburgh's urban housing to more salient public attention. On the Royal Mile, tenement numbers 99 and 103 suddenly rumbled then collapsed in an explosion of brickwork. The tenements were 250 years old, and the effects of another winter proved too much for the structures. Thirty-five people were killed almost instantaneously, but as rescuers dragged through the rubble, expecting no survivors, they heard a voice: 'Heave awa' lads, I'm no deid yet!' The voice came from a young boy, Joseph McIvor – the only survivor. Joseph's story, and the dreadful death toll, prompted greater public reaction. The tenements were rebuilt and graced with a carving of McIvor on the lintel with his words inscribed above (although 'lads' was replace by 'chaps' for the benefit of English visitors).

Arrival of the Trams

By the second half of the nineteenth century, many cities in the United Kingdom were buying into the use of trams as a way of giving the population mobility. For Edinburgh, the arrival of the trams came in 1871 with the foundation of the Edinburgh Street Tramways Company. The early trams run by the company were horse-drawn, but by 1899 cable-powered trams were introduced, mostly built by Brown Marshall and Electric Railway & Tramway Carriage Works Ltd, although some were constructed by local enthusiasts. Routes also expanded to take in more of the city. The next stage in the city's transport evolution was the introduction of electrically powered trams. Electric trams spread through the United Kingdom during the last years of the nineteenth century and the first two decades of the twentieth century. Edinburgh received her first electric tram in 1905, which was unveiled with the official opening of Leith Corporation Tramways on 3 November. In 1907 the last of the horse-drawn trams were finally phased out, and by 1922 electrically powered trams had entirely replaced cable trams. These provided a through route from Edinburgh to Leith that did not require a change of trams at any point.

Trams ran in Edinburgh, with numerous upgrades, until 1956. By that year motor vehicles were the future, and trams (felt to be a cause of congestion) were replaced with buses on all routes. Three trams were paraded through the streets on 16 November to mark the passing. However, at the time of writing Edinburgh is once again planning to reintroduce trams in an attempt, ironically, to reduce the city's congestion.

James Clerk Maxwell (1831-79)

James Clerk Maxwell was an acute scientific mind of the late nineteenth century, a mind that had its formative years amongst Edinburgh's academic establishments. Maxwell was an Edinburgh man born and bred. He was born at 14 India Street and showed a precocious intelligence from his earliest years. Maxwell attended the Edinburgh Academy from 1841, and by the age of 14 he was already exploring higher-level mathematics and published his first scientific paper when he was only 15. In 1847 Maxwell entered the University of Edinburgh, where he published two more scientific papers and obtained entrance into Peterhouse College, Cambridge, in 1850, quickly moving to Trinity College.

Maxwell graduated from Trinity in 1854 with a degree in mathematics, but this was only the start of an exceptional academic career in both mathematics and physics. He subsequently became professor at Marischal College in Aberdeen and King's College in London, and in 1871 became the first

Cavendish Professor of Physics at Cambridge. (He also unsuccessfully applied for a position at the University of Edinburgh.) Maxwell is principally remembered for his work on theories relating to gases and electromagnetism. His work on gases explored the molecular mechanisms of temperature, and his conclusions took the study of thermodynamics in exciting new directions. Maxwell's studies on electromagnetism between 1864 and 1873 made important refinements to the understanding of electromagnetic radiation and how electricity could be used to provide magnetic effects. Maxwell did further important work in many scientific areas, although clung to his religious faith in a created universe. He died at the age of only 48 from stomach cancer.

Edinburgh International Exhibition

The nineteenth century was a time in which all parts of Britain wished to show off the might of empire and industry, and the city of Edinburgh was no exception. There was a vogue for large-scale exhibitions, and in 1886 Edinburgh unveiled its own International Exhibition of Industry, Science and Art on the Meadows.

Opened by Prince Albert Victor, the Exhibition was a truly huge undertaking. The venue consisted of a large Grand Hall (spacious enough for 10,000 people) with double courts extending outwards from the rear. Inside was a huge diversity of exhibits – over 20,000 in total – with objects brought in from all over the British empire. Listed exhibits included 'educational appliances; Italian furniture and marble; violins from Prague; Turkish embroidery; illustrations of mining, pottery, sugar-

Queen Victoria leaving Holyrood Palace after her visit to the city in 1886

refining, sea industries, paper-making, printing; and railway, tram-way and other vehicular appliances'. There was also an 'Old Edinburgh Street', a full-size representation of a seventeenth-century Edinburgh thoroughfare, including a copy of the Old Tolbooth. Outside were rockeries and gardens, and even an electric railway that ran throughout the exhibition grounds.

The Edinburgh International Exhibition was a stunning success, and in total some 30,000 people passed through the event, including Queen Victoria herself, who visited in August. At the end of the Exhibition, however, every building and structure was pulled down and removed, although various bits and pieces can be found dotted around modern Edinburgh as a reminder.

Robert Louis Stevenson (1850-94)

Few Edinburgh luminaries carry the worldwide recognition of Robert Louis Stevenson. His verses, fiction and essays are some of the most famous in the English language, and include *Treasure Island* (1883), *The Strange Case Of Dr Jekyll And Mr Hyde* (1886), *Virginibus Puerisque* (1881) and *Kidnapped* (1886). His vision for themes and gift for storytelling still compel us today, and yet it was his early life in Edinburgh that provided him with much of the material for his later work.

Stevenson was born on 13 November 1850 in Howard Place near Edinburgh New Town. He was a sickly child and would grow to be physically weak adult – a fact that partly explains his constant roaming abroad in later life to find healthier climates. One of Stevenson's nurses, Alison Cunningham, used to tell the young boy passionate tales of the religious wars of the seventeenth-century Covenanters, imbuing Stevenson with the love of storytelling. In fact, Stevenson's first publication was a pamphlet on the Battle of Rullion Green of 1666. The Stevensons moved several times within the New Town to try to find more salubrious housing for their son, eventually ending up at 17 Heriot Row. Stevenson was educated at Edinburgh Academy then Edinburgh University, where he trained to be an engineer like his father. (For a short time he was editor of the Edinburgh University magazine.) Although he was promising in this role, he eventually switched to law and in 1875 was admitted to the Scottish Bar. From the mid-1870s, however, his literary output was prolific and he began to travel widely to destinations such as Europe and the South Pacific. He ended his days living a long way from the city of his birth, and died in Samoa on 3 December 1894.

Urban Expansion

The need for Edinburgh to expand its physical size has been a recurrent theme throughout its history. Surges in population have forced urban growth within the city, first upwards (with the high-rise tenement system of the Old Town) and then outwards (with New Town and suburban developments). Expansion was once again on the cards in the early decades of the twentieth century, as Scotland's population became increasingly urbanized. By 1911, a full 30 per cent of Scotland's entire population was living in either Edinburgh, Glasgow, Dundee or

Aberdeen, up from 22 per cent 50 years previously. In Edinburgh, the only way to cope with such a surge of population was to grow outwards, displacing more and more of the population from the centre to the peripheries. In fact, the Old and New Towns went into something of a decline as the outwards growth pulled more of the money for development.

The city's growth continued the development of many of Edinburgh's bustling suburbs, such as Dunningston and Craigmillar to the south-east, Morningside to the south and Granton to the north-west. Eventually the expansion fused Edinburgh and Leith in one seamless urban spread, leading to the amalgamation of the two town councils in 1920. Although the expansion undoubtedly brought its tensions, it also provided a better quality of housing for many than was available in the heart of the city. That remains true for many people today, and like all cities of the United Kingdom, Edinburgh is surrounded by a bustling commuter belt.

James Connolly (1868–1916)

James Connolly is forever associated with modern Irish history, but it was Edinburgh in which he was born and spent his developmental years. He was born on 5 June 1868 in the Cowgate area. Like many of Edinburgh's citizens at the end of the nineteenth century, Connolly's parents were Irish immigrants who arrived in Scotland in the 1850s. Life was extremely hard for the young Connolly. His mother died when he was young, living conditions were poor and he had to cope with the prevalent anti-Irish feeling in the city at the time. His first job was working in the print room for the Edinburgh *Evening News*, then in 1882 he joined the British Army, in which he witnessed the suppression of Irish people while deployed in Ireland. In 1889 he left the Army and returned to Edinburgh, becoming a carter then a cobbler, but he also embraced socialism and founded/joined various socialist and Irish nationalist organizations within the city, becoming secretary of the Scottish Socialist Federation.

Eventually Connolly left Edinburgh for Dublin where in 1896 he founded the Irish Socialist Republican Society. Connolly's socialist passion and eloquence took him on a lecture tour of America, and on his return to Ireland he became a radical union leader and, eventually, a determined supporter of Irish independence. During the Easter Rising of 1916 he was appointed the commander of Republican forces in the city, a role that proved to be his downfall. On 12 May 1916, having been wounded and captured by the British, Connolly was executed by firing squad, his body dumped into a mass grave.

Elsie Inglis (1864-1917)

Elsie Inglis is one of those rare individuals who swam against the tide of an entire society, and achieved great humanitarian achievements while doing so. She was born in India in 1864, the daughter of a civil servant, and was encouraged to pursue an education from her earliest days. The family moved to Edinburgh and the young Inglis set her heart on a medical career. Her initial training took place at the Edinburgh School of Medicine for Women established by another impressive Victorian woman,

Dr Sophie Jex Blake, and she furthered her studies at the Edinburgh Medical College and the Glasgow Royal Infirmary.

Inglis qualified as a doctor in 1892 and went to work in London, where she discovered less than ideal care of female patients, particularly those undergoing problems with maternity. She was a headstrong woman, and in 1894 she returned to Edinburgh where, along with another female doctor, she established a specialist maternity hospital for the poor on the High Street. Staffed entirely by women, the hospital was a compassionate and forward-thinking institution, and it eventually became the Elsie Inglis Memorial Hospital.

Inglis was as much a political as a medical campaigner, and became very vocal in the Scottish suffragette movement – she founded the Scottish Women's Suffragette Federation in 1906. It was this organization that went on to send medical teams to some of the worst battlezones of the First World War, and Inglis herself served in France, Serbia and Russia. Yet her punishing life was taking its toll, and she returned to the United Kingdom suffering from cancer in October 1917. She died a month later, and was buried in her beloved Edinburgh, in Dean Cemetery.

The Scottish National War Memorial

A total of 150,000 young Scotsmen were killed during World War I. As in many cities around the United Kingdom, the grief for such loss found expression in Edinburgh with the erection of a war memorial. The idea for a specifically Scottish memorial came in 1917, and was proposed by a group of influential military and civic leaders led by John George, 8th Duke of Atholl (1871–1942). Debate raged over where to locate the memorial, and in October 1918 a Scottish National War Memorial Committee was formed by the government to consider the issue, with Captain George Swinton (1859–1937) acting as secretary.

The chosen site for the memorial was Edinburgh Castle, and after much deliberation and public argument it was decided to convert the North Barracks, known as the Billings Barracks after the conversion work of Robert Billings there in the 1860s. In April 1918 the architect Robert Lorimer (1884–1929) was appointed to convert the barracks into a memorial. He proposed a memorial shrine, a seemingly innocuous suggestion that nonetheless encountered fierce opposition (many protested in terms of the cost or the modifications to the castle). In 1923, however, building work began.

Work was finally completed in 1927, with the opening ceremony conducted by the Prince of Wales on 14 July. Thousands of visitors subsequently, and to this day, flocked to the shrine to pay their respects and look at the names of relatives and loved ones on the Rolls of Honour. Sadly, the National War Memorial would have more work to do – 50,000 additional names were added to the Rolls of Honour following World War II.

Sir Patrick Geddes (1854–1932)

Sir Patrick Geddes was an academic who, unlike many in his profession, actually tackled real world issues. He was born in Ballater, Aberdeenshire, on 2 October 1854. His first job as a young man was working in the National Bank of Scotland, but his real love was science and he entered Edinburgh University to study botany. Although he would remain deeply interested in botany for the rest of his life, and in several other sciences and arts, he is primarily remembered for his work in town planning, a subject about which he became passionate from the early 1880s. (He was nevertheless eventually appointed the Professor of Botany at the University of Dundee, having been rejected by Edinburgh on account of his radical social views.) Geddes argued, with much insight and prescience, that the environment in which people lived had a deep effect over their psychological and social development. He was appalled by the conditions of people living in Edinburgh's slum areas, which he often observed from the camera obscura in the Outlook Tower at the top of the Royal Mile.

Geddes put his theories into practice, overseeing the design of places such as Ramsay Gardens, Blackie House and the Scottish National Zoological Park. He also worked extensively abroad, working in India, Palestine and France. He is rightly known as one of the fathers of modern urban planning.

The Edinburgh International Festival

The post-World War II period in Britain was one of general austerity, but the city of Edinburgh managed to shed a little light on the gloom with the development of the Edinburgh International Festival (EIF). It was founded by a group of artistic and civic leaders who, in their own words, wanted to create an annual event that would 'provide a platform for the flowering of the human spirit'. The key individuals behind this enterprise were Rudolf Bing, the General Manager of Glyndebourne Opera, Henry Harvey Wood, the Head of the British Council in Scotland, and several other influential figures in the city's administration. The basic intention was for a cultural event that would promote the best of music, theatre and opera, and at the same time fuel the tourism that would be so important to the city's post-war reconstruction.

The first festival was held in 1947, and continues to run to this day, showcasing some of the best artistic talent in the world. Yet the EIF is far from the only festival or annual cultural event in Edinburgh. In 1950, the first Edinburgh Military Tattoo was held, a celebration of Scottish, British and international military heritage that to date has been visited by over 100 million people. Equally as famous, but far more irreverent, is the sprawling Edinburgh Festival Fringe, also established in 1947. 'The Fringe' developed as a less formal alternative to the main festival (it was created by eight theatre companies that attended the first festival uninvited), and has today grown into one of the city's landmark events, known particularly for its off-beat drama, comedy, dance and music, all loosely choreographed between several hundred venues. The combined festivals have not only given Edinburgh a massive tourist boost, they have also given it a clear cultural identity.

Clearing the Slums

In the aftermath of World War II, Edinburgh's town council was forced to face up to some unpleasant truths about its city. Although the days of 'Auld Reekie' were long gone, there remained a large section of the city's population that was still living in substandard slum housing. Victorian tenements in places such as Carnegie Street and St Leonard's and Dumbiedykes were in a terrible condition, and provided damp, cold and unpleasant housing for its inhabitants. In the late 1950s and 1960s, a major programme of slum clearance was implemented. Entire streets of terraced tenements were demolished, and the occupants displaced to alternative accommodation. At first that accommodation was post-war prefab housing, but gradually council house and flats became available. Then came the curse of the 1960s – high-rise tower blocks. Numerous blocks sprung up around Edinburgh in places such as Blackhall, Slateford, Gracemount and Leith. The largest example was at Muirfield – 23 storeys tall. Those places not graced with tower blocks were provided with large estates.

The irony was that the council had replaced historical slums with potential slums of the future. By the 1970s and 1980s, many of the estates and tower blocks had degenerated into decay and criminality, and it is no surprise that many tower blocks have been demolished in recent years.

The Stone of Destiny

On 15 November 1996, amidst great ceremony, the British government of John Major transferred a large block of red sandstone back into Scottish hands. It was reverentially transported back to Edinburgh and installed on display in Edinburgh Castle. This was the so-called 'Stone of Destiny', or more awkwardly, 'Stone of Scone' (after the place where it was principally located), one of the most sacred relics of Scottish history.

The veneration of the Stone begins well back into the medieval period, as it was used during enthronement ceremonies of numerous Scottish monarchs (the monarchs were seated upon the stone during their coronation). The legends of its sacred origins are numerous and frequently contradictory, but the Stone certainly became an emblem of Scottish national identity, which made many English monarchs eager to get their hands on it. In 1296 the worst happened, as it was captured by Edward I during his wars with the Scots and was taken back to Westminster Abbey in London. There it would stay for 700 years, fixed beneath the seat of a wooden coronation chair on which almost every English monarch has been crowned. Its only adventure during this time was when a group of Scottish students stole it in 1950, managing to break it in two in the process. The Stone was eventually recovered and repaired, but in 1996 it was decided that it should rightfully reside in Scotland.

Scottish Parliament

In 1997, the Labour Party under Tony Blair swept the Conservatives out of office, and ushered in a distinctive period of politics in the United Kingdom. One of the principles underlying the 'New Labour' philosophy was a respect for regional differences, and the strong desire in countries such as Scotland and Wales for a greater measure of self-government. Clamour for a Scottish parliament specifically had been sharp from the 1960s onwards, and following a referendum held in September 1997 such a wish was granted – Scotland was to have an independent parliament with some tax-varying powers, confirmed with the passing of the Scotland Act 1998.

The new Scottish Parliament was elected on 6 May 1996, and had its first sitting six days later. Some of the opening words came from the chair, Dr Winnie Ewing, who said, 'I have the opportunity to make a short speech and I want to begin with the words that I have always wanted either to say or to hear someone else say: the Scottish Parliament, which adjourned on 25 March 1707, is hereby reconvened.'

Initially the Parliament was held in the Church of Scotland Assembly Halls while a new, ultra-modern building designed by the Catalan architect Enric Miralles was designed in the Holyrood area. This was finally opened (after much turmoil over spiralling budgets) by the Queen on 9 October 2004. After Edinburgh's long and frequently brutal political history, and a lengthy yearning for self-government, the opening of the official Scottish Parliament building was an emotional moment for many.

The Drive for Independence

And yet, the drive for self-government persists. A historic referendum took place on 18 September 2014, which asked the Scottish people whether Scotland should be an independent country. The 'No' side won by 5.3% of the vote, after a huge 84.6% turnout. However, following the 'yes' result in another nationwide referendum in June 2016, this time asking if the UK should leave the EU, in this largely pro-EU country there has been renewed momentum for a second Scottish independence referendum. Scottish MPs are to debate First Minister Nicola Sturgeon's plan to to ask Westminster for permission to hold a referendum. Edinburgh may yet become the capital of an independent country.

Glossary

Act of Union

The 1707 Act or Treaty of Union, which established a single British state: the United Kingdom of Great Britain. The union abolished the Scottish Parliament and transferred political sovereignty to a new British Parliament.

Age of Enlightenment

A Europe-wide phenomenon and a time of accelerated learning and a breaking free from previous theological confines of knowledge into new areas of science, literature, economics and philosophy.

Angles of Northumbria

A Germanic-speaking people allied with the Romans, who defeated King Oswald to take over the fortified settlement of Dunedin.

Auld Alliance

A Franco-Scottish treaty signed in 1295 that allied the two countries together in a mutual defence pact against English expansionism. Both countries were bound to a reciprocal arrangement that held until 1560.

Auld Reekie

A Scottish phrase meaning 'Old Stinky', and the nickname given to the city's Old Town. Specifically refers to the unimaginable living conditions during the sixteenth century.

Black Death

A form of bubonic plague that spread throughout Europe and Asia from the fourteenth century, killing over 50 million people.

Blue Blanket

The name of the banner conferred to Edinburgh's trades people by King James III in 1482.

Bronze Age

Period between the Stone Age and Iron Age lasting in Scotland from about 2,000 BC to 500 BC, during which time weapons and tools were made of bronze.

Burgh

Scottish word for borough. The 'burgh' in Edinburgh meaning 'fortress' or 'walled buildings'.

Burial Cairn

An artificial pile of stones, often in a conical form, built to mark a burial site or grave.

Covenanters

A group of extreme Presbyterians who raised armies against Charles I in the seventeenth century in order to defend their doctrine of extreme absolutism.

Dunedin (or Din Eidin)

Names given to the area now known as Edinburgh at the time of the Votadini tribe.

Glorious Revolution

The Revolution of 1688, in which King James VII of Scotland was forced from office and fled to France, and the throne was occupied by William III and Mary II of England.

Gododdin

The name given by the early Britons to the descendents of the Votadini tribe who had inhabited the Edinburgh area from the Iron Age.

Golden Charter

The name of the royal charter given to the city of Edinburgh by James III, giving the city magistrates more local law-making powers. Another golden charter was given in 1603 by James VI, which extended the city's legal jurisdiction over Leith and Newhaven.

The Great Cause

The political situation arising in 1291 after the death of Princess Margaret, Maid of Norway, leaving no obvious heir to the Scottish throne. Refers to the settlement of the dispute between John Balliol and Robert the Bruce, two primary claimants to the throne, as to who should rule Scotland.

Iron Age

Period following the Bronze Age, c. 500 BC, which was characterized by the rapid spread of iron tools and weapons.

Jacobites

Supporters of King James VII/II, who rose up against William III of

England after the Glorious Revolution of 1688, carrying out acts of rebellion during the rule of his successors.

The Killing Times

The period of violence following the restoration of Charles II and his renewed attempts to bring Episcopalianism to Scotland. Rebellions by Covenanters resulted in many battles with government troops as the government sought to eradicate rebellious factions. The killings continued until the death of Charles II in 1685.

Kirk

Scottish word for church.

The Lang Siege

The term given to a siege of Edinburgh Castle that ran from 1571–73. James Douglas, 4th Earl of Morton, the regent during the minority of James VI, battled to reclaim the castle from Sir William Kirkaldy of Grange, a noble ally of Mary, Queen of Scots.

Lord Provost

The title given to the city's figurative and ceremonial civic head. It is an ancient office dating back to the thirteenth century.

Lords of Session

The title given to the 15 members of the Court of Session, Scotland's supreme civil court founded in 1532 by James V. James wanted a permanent and authoritative legal body to oversee cases of royal and social importance, and to act as a form of appeal court.

Lords of the Congregation

A collection of powerful Scottish nobles who began a programme of destruction targeting Edinburgh's Romanist buildings during the Scottish Reformation.

Mercat Cross

Mercat crosses are found in cities, towns and villages across Scotland, and historically mark the places where markets would gather for trading. Edinburgh's Mercat Cross was also the site of public announcements and public executions.

National Covenant

Defining document of the Covenanting Revolution drawn up by leading members of the Scottish clergy in 1638. Created in response to Charles I's major programme of religious reform, including the introduction of a new prayer book and the imposition of Episcopacy. A landmark act of resistance against English rule.

Picts

A confederation of tribes that occupied the area that is now central and northern Scotland at the time of the Romans until the tenth century. After moving south they established a fortress on the site of Edinburgh Castle.

The Renaissance

A period of intellectual and commercial expansion for much of Europe. Edinburgh thrived under the hands of a series of authoritarian monarchs, from James II to James IV, and expanded in both size and prosperity, spurred on by new forms of industry and a growth in population.

The Restoration
The return of King Charles II to his British kingdoms in 1660 after his political exile during the Cromwellian ascendancy and military occupation.

The Rough Wooing
A military campaign ordered by England's King Henry VIII in 1544 in an attempt to forcefully persuade the Scottish court to allow his son Edward to marry the infant Scottish queen, Mary. A violent, yet unsuccessful attempt to forge an alliance between England and Scotland that destroyed much of the city.

The Scottish Reformation
The Reformation of the Church in 1560, which saw the foundation of the Church of Scotland. Catholic mass was prohibited, the jurisdiction of the Pope was banned, and authority was given to a Protestant Confession of Faith.

Tolbooth
An administrative centre at which tolls were collected. Edinburgh's 'Auld Tolbooth' was used for an array of civic roles, including being home to the high court and national Parliament, and serving as the city's civic headquarters, tax office and prison.

Union of Crowns
The union of England and Scotland after the death of Queen Elizabeth I of England in 1603. James VI of Scotland inherited the English throne and was crowned James I of England.

Votadini

A people of the Iron Age, whose territory ranged from south-east Scotland to north-east England, from the Firth of Forth down to the River Tyne. There is evidence that sometime around 400 BC they shifted their centre of power to Dunedin, what is today the Edinburgh area.

Wynd

Scottish word for a narrow lane or alley commonly used when referring to the streets of Edinburgh's Old Town.

West side of Charlotte Square, showing St George's Church

Further Reading

Anderson, J., A History of Edinburgh from the Earliest Period to the Completion of the Half Century 1850, A. Fullarton & Co., Edinburgh, 1856

Anderson, R. et al, The University of Edinburgh: An Illustrated History, Edinburgh University Press, Edinburgh, 2003

Bold, A., Scotland: A Literary Guide, Routledge, London, 1989

Buchan, J., Capital of the Mind: How Edinburgh Changed the World, John Murray, London, 2003

Campbell, D., Edinburgh: A Cultural and Literary History, Signal Books, Oxford, 2003

Coghill, H., A Century of Edinburgh: Events, People and Places of the Twentieth Century, Sutton Publishing, Stroud, 2007

Coghill, H., Lost Edinburgh: Edinburgh's Lost Architectural Heritage, Birlinn, Edinburgh, 2005

Daiches, D. (ed.), A Traveller's Companion to Edinburgh, Constable & Robinson, London, 2004

Donaldson, G., The Edinburgh History of Scotland: James V–James VII, Mercat Press, Edinburgh, 1975

Edwards, B. and Jenkins, P., Edinburgh: The Making of a Capital City, Edinburgh University Press, Edinburgh, 2005

Fitzpatrick, K., Edinburgh: An Illustrated Journey, Flame Tree Publishing, London, 2005

Harris, S., The Place Names of Edinburgh, Steve Savage, London, 1996

Houston, R.A. (ed) and Knox, W. (ed), The New Penguin History of Scotland: From the Earliest Times to the Present Day, Penguin Books, London, 2002

Lochead, M., *Edinburgh Lore and Legend* Robert Hale, London, 1986

Lynch, M. (ed), *Oxford Companion to Scottish History*, Oxford University Press, Oxford, 2007

Mackay, J. (ed), *Pocket Scottish History*, Parragon Books, Bath, 2002

Magnusson, M., *Scotland: The Story of a Nation*, HarperCollins Publishers, London, 2001

McKean, C., *Edinburgh: Portrait of a City*, Century, London, 1991

Potter, H., *Edinburgh Under Siege, 1571–73*, NPI Media Group, Stroud, 2003

Wallace, J.M., *The Historic Houses of Edinburgh* John Donald, Edinburgh, 1998

Youngerson, A.J., *The Companion Guide to Edinburgh and the Borders*, Polygon, Edinburgh, 2001

Youngerson, A.J., *The Making of Classical Edinburgh, 1750–1840*, Edinburgh University Press, Edinburgh, 2002

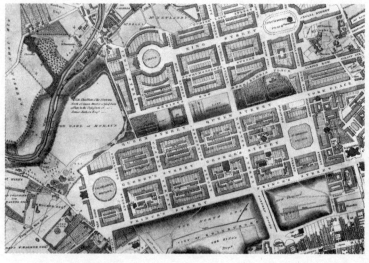

James Craig's plans for the New Town, 1767

Author Biographies

Dr Christopher McNab (author)

Dr Christopher McNab is a writer and editor, based in South Wales but with a long-standing affection for Edinburgh and family roots in Scotland. Since completing a PhD in English and Cultural Theory at the University of Wales Aberystwyth, Chris has published over 25 books internationally and has written for numerous magazines and encyclopedias. Although Chris specializes in adult general history and military history, he has also penned many publications for children, on subject matter ranging from ships to dinosaurs. Titles that Chris has written in whole or part include *Reformation, Exploration and Empire, World's Greatest Historical Disasters, The Illustrated History of the Vietnam War* and *Tools of Violence.*

John McKay (foreword)

Scottish writer and film-maker, born 1964, John McKay grew up in East Lothian and studied at Edinburgh University. It was here that he co-founded the celebrated Scots theatre and comedy troupe The Merry Mac Fun Co., and wrote plays for the Traverse Theatre and other Scottish companies, including *Dead Dad Dog* and *My Brother's Keeper.* Film and TV includes *Crush, The Canterbury Tales, Life on Mars* and the Edinburgh-set *Reichenbach Falls.*

Index

British Institute 160
Bronze Age 14, 22
Broomhouse 22
Brown Marshall and Electric
    Railway & Tramway Carriage
    Works Ltd 189
Bruce, Robert 98–99, 110
Burgh Muir 108
burghs 37, 43, 51
Burke, William 179–81
Burn, William 36
Burns, Robert 138, 155–56

C
Calton Hill 15, 164, 187
Calvin, John 73
Campbell, Archibald, 3rd Duke of
    Argyll 150–51
Campbell, Archibald, Marquis
    of Argyll 14, 36, 113, 116–17,
    121, 145
Canongate 14, 15, 112, 114, 126
    Kirk of the Canongate 38
Canonmills 173, 182
Carberry Hill 83, 85
Carham 30–31
Carnegie Street 201
Castle Rock 13, 16, 23, 24, 141
Castlehill 147, 150
Chambers, Robert 53–54, 128
Chambers, Sir William 186
Charles I 18, 36, 102–103, 104–105,
    106, 110–11, 112, 113, 114,
    117–18, 119

Charles II 36, 106, 112–13,
    118–19, 166
    Restoration 115–16
Charles X of France 63
cholera outbreak 168–69
Christian I of Denmark-Norway 60
city walls 57–58
class divide 136–37
Cleaning the Causeway 69–70
Comyn, John 46–47
Connolly, James 195–96
Cook, Robin 88
Corbett, Ronnie 39
Court of Session (Court of Justice)
    71, 103
Courts of Justice 90–91
Covenanters 14, 102–103, 112, 113,
    116–19
Cowgate 56, 103, 140, 195
Craig, James 133
Craigleith Quarry 165
Craigmillar 195
Cromwell, Oliver 96, 103, 106, 112,
    113, 114–15, 116, 117, 118, 166
Crossrig, Lord 125
Cullen, William 138
Culloden 132
Cumberland 41
Cumberland, Duke of 132
Cunningham, Alison 194

D
Darien venture 126, 129
Darnley, Lord 77, 79–80, 81, 85